Be prepared...
To learn...
To succeed...

READY, SET, GO!®

NJ ASK
Language Arts Literacy
Grade 4

Staff of Research & Education Association
Piscataway, New Jersey

Research & Education Association
Visit our website at
www.rea.com

The Performance Standards in this book were created and implemented by the New Jersey State Department of Education. For further information, visit the Department of Education website at *www.state.nj.us/njded/cccs.*

Research & Education Association
61 Ethel Road West
Piscataway, New Jersey 08854
E-mail: info@rea.com

Ready, Set, Go!®
New Jersey ASK
Language Arts Literacy
Grade 4

Published 2012
Copyright © 2010 by Research & Education Association, Inc.
Prior edition copyright © 2007 by Research & Education Association, Inc.
All rights reserved. No part of this book may be reproduced in any form without permission of the publisher.

Printed in the United States of America

Library of Congress Control Number 2009940387

ISBN-13: 978-0-7386-0798-6
ISBN-10: 0-7386-0798-3

Contents

Section 2: Writing

Section 3: Practice Tests

Section 4: Answer Keys

About Research & Education Association

Founded in 1959, Research & Education Association (REA) is dedicated to publishing the finest and most effective educational materials—including software, study guides, and test preps—for students in elementary school, middle school, high school, college, graduate school, and beyond.

Today REA's wide-ranging catalog is a leading resource for teachers, students, and professionals.

We invite you to visit us at *www.rea.com* to find out how "REA is making the world smarter."

Acknowledgments

We would like to thank REA's Larry B. Kling, Vice President, Editorial, for supervising development; Pam Weston, Vice President, Publishing, for setting the quality standards for production integrity and managing the publication to completion; Alice Leonard, Senior Editor, for project management, editorial guidance, and preflight editorial review of the new edition; Diane Goldschmidt, Senior Editor, and Molly Solanki, Associate Editor, for post-production quality assurance; Rachel DiMatteo, Graphic Artist, for her design contributions; and Christine Saul, Senior Graphic Artist, for cover design.

We also gratefully acknowledge the writers, educators, and editors of REA and Northeast Editing for content development, editorial guidance, and final review. Thanks to Kelly Brownlee for her wonderful illustrations and to Matrix Publishing for page design and typesetting. We would like to thank NUW Editorial Services and MediaLynx for their assistance with this edition.

Introduction

Welcome to an Educational Adventure

The NJ ASK is the Garden State's answer to the federal No Child Left Behind Act, which requires that states use standards-based testing to ensure that students are gaining the skills and knowledge necessary for academic success.

We at REA believe that a friendly, hands-on introduction and preparation for the test are the means to creating a successful experience. REA's NJ ASK books offer these key features:

✓ Clearly identified book activities

✓ Contextual illustrations

✓ Easy-to-follow lessons

✓ Step-by-step examples

✓ Tips for solving problems tailored to each grade level

✓ Exercises to sharpen skills

✓ Real practice

On the next page you will find information for students, parents, and teachers regarding the NJ ASK in particular and test-taking in general. Organized practice with the components of the test will allow students to hone skills that, in turn, will set the tone for success all along their educational adventures. It is REA's hope that this book—by providing relevant, standards-based practice—can become an integral part of that adventure.

What is the NJ ASK?*

The New Jersey Assessment of Skills and Knowledge is a standards-based assessment. The Grade 4 test was redesigned in 2009 to include more rigorous and diverse content, and to provide a better sense of whether students are on track to advance to the next level in their educational journey. Specifically, performance on the NJ ASK measures how well students have acquired the knowledge and skills outlined in the state's Core Curriculum Content Standards. Those measures fall into three broad categories, or bands: "partially proficient," "proficient," and "advanced proficient."

When is the NJ ASK given?

The test is administered in early spring. Grade 4 students take the test on five mornings, the first two in Language Arts Literacy, the next two mornings in Mathematics, and the last in Science. Test length spans from 60 to 90 minutes, depending on the subject.

What is the format of the NJ ASK?

The NJ ASK has two types of questions: multiple choice and open ended. For multiple choice, students are asked to choose the correct answer from four choices. For open-ended questions, children answer with written responses in their own words. Each test section is timed, and students may not proceed to the next section until time for the current section has expired. If students have not finished a section when time runs out, they must stop and put down their pencils. There are clear directions throughout the test.

Understanding the NJ ASK and This Book
Students:

This book was specially written and designed to make test practice easy and rewarding. Our practice tests are very much like the actual NJ ASK tests, and our review is filled with illustrations, drills, exercises, and practice questions to help you become familiar with the testing environment and to retain information about key topics.

---

* Source: New Jersey Assessment of Skills and Knowledge, *2009 Score Interpretation Manual, Grades 3-8:* October 2009: Copyright © New Jersey Department of Education

Parents:

The NJ ASK is designed to give schools information about how well students have acquired the knowledge and skills outlined in the state's Core Curriculum Content Standards (CCCS). These standards describe what students should know and be able to do at the end of each grade. This book will help your child review and prepare effectively and positively for the NJ ASK in Language Arts Literacy.

Teachers:

The Practice Tests in this book include the number of passages, items, and prompts that are used to gauge whether students are at, above, or below proficiency levels. The actual NJ ASK test forms, however, will also contain content being field tested for use on future tests. Thus, students will likely find themselves answering more questions than are featured in the Practice Tests at the end of this book.

The new writing prompts are also based on the National Assessment of Educational Progress (NAEP) 2011 Writing Frameworks as well as the NJ CCCS.

As their teacher, you introduce your students to the test-taking environment and the demands of the NJ ASK tests. You can use our authoritative book in your classroom for planned, guided instruction, and practice testing. Effective preparation means better test scores!

Where can I obtain more information about the NJ ASK?

For more information about the NJ ASK, contact the New Jersey Department of Education or Measurement Inc.:

www.state.nj.us/education/assessment   www.measinc.com/njask

Office of Evaluation and Assessment
Telephone: 609-292-4469
Mailing Address:
New Jersey Department of Education
PO Box 500
Trenton, NJ 08625-05000

For more information on the National Assessment of Educational Progress (NAEP) Writing Frameworks:

http://nagb.org/publications/frameworks.htm

Test Accommodations and Special Situations

Every effort is made to provide a level playing field for students with disabilities who are taking the NJ ASK. Most students with educational disabilities and most students whose English language skills are limited take the standard NJ ASK. Students with disabilities will be working toward achieving the standards at whatever level is appropriate for them. Supports such as large-print type are available for students who have a current Individualized Education Program (IEP) or who have plans required under Section 504 or who use these supports and accommodations during other classroom testing.

If the IEP team decides that a student will not take the NJ ASK in Language Arts Literacy, Mathematics, and/or Science, the child will take the Alternate Proficiency Assessment (APA).

Tips for Test Taking

- **Do your homework.** From the first assignment of the year, organize the day so there is always time to study and keep up with homework.

- **Communicate.** If there are any questions, doubts, or concerns about anything relating to school, study, or tests, speak up. This goes for teachers and parents, as well as students.

- **Get some rest.** Getting a good night's sleep the night before the test is essential to waking up sharp and focused.

- **Eat right.** Having a good breakfast—nothing very heavy—the morning of the test is what the body and mind need. Comfortable clothes, plenty of time to get to school, and the confidence of having prepared properly are all any student needs.

- **Test smart.** Read the questions carefully. Make sure answers are written correctly in the proper place on the answer sheet. Don't rush, and don't go too slow. If there is time, go back and check questions that you weren't sure about.

Format of the NJ ASK Language Arts Literacy Test

The NJ ASK Language Arts Literacy Test is administered over two days. The writing portion of the test requires students to write two essays in response to two expository prompts. The reading portion contains three passages with a total of 27 multiple-choice questions and three open-ended questions. In each test, students alternate between generating their own texts (writing) and analyzing texts written by others (reading).

Text Type/Strand	Task	Time
Writing: Expository prompts (2)	Compositions	30 minutes each test session
Reading: Narrative and Everyday text (3 passages)	9 multiple-choice and 1 open-ended per passage	60 minutes each test session

The actual NJ ASK test forms will also contain additional content that is being field tested for use on future tests. Thus, students will be answering more questions than are featured in the Practice Tests at the end of this book.

Reading

For the NJ ASK, **narrative text** is defined as literature written primarily to tell a story. These passages have a conflict and address common aspects of human nature. For grade 4, narrative passages of between 500 and 1,000 words are selected from previously published literature. Narrative passages chosen for the NJ ASK contain the following elements:

- Significant themes that are age appropriate and grade-level appropriate
- A clearly identifiable problem/conflict and resolution
- A well-organized plot with clearly developed and meaningful events
- Well-developed characters
- Settings integral to the plot
- Literary elements, such as imagery and foreshadowing
- A range of vocabulary for which adequate context is provided

On the NJ ASK, **everyday text** is defined as text that people encounter in their daily lives. It is designed to convey information about a topic and/or show how to do something. Everyday texts of varying formats are selected and/or adapted from previously published sources such as magazine, newspapers, how-to books, and hands-on activity kits and workbooks. Everyday texts range in length from 400 to 900 words. The text has a strong central idea or purpose and contains the following elements:

- Engaging topics that are age- and grade-level appropriate

- A clear, positive focus

- A clearly developed explanation of ideas, activities, or action

- A clearly developed sequence of ideas, activities, or actions

- Performable activities or actions

- Vivid and clear illustrations

- A range of vocabulary for which adequate context is provided

Writing

The **expository writing task** can take one of two forms. One form is based on a poem that is read aloud by the examiner as the students read silently. Students then respond to a written prompt that extends an idea introduced by the poem. The other expository prompt form is a simple, written prompt based on familiar topics that asks students to describe, discuss, explain, or analyze some aspect of the topic. Students are able to draw on their personal experience and knowledge to develop ideas for their compositions.

Each writing test provides space for students to plan their ideas. Students are encouraged to use a prewriting strategy (e.g., making a web, a list or some other sort of graphic organizer) of their choosing to organize their thoughts. The instructions direct students to write their own story or composition on the lined pages provided. This version of their writing is considered a first draft.

Each writing task is administered in a consistent format and in a constant time segment of 30 minutes. Students are instructed to use the first few minutes to develop ideas for their writing and to use the last few minutes to review and revise what they have written.

Scoring the Test

On the reading portion of the Grade 4 NJ ASK, each of the 27 multiple-choice questions is worth 1 point. Open-ended questions are scored holistically on a 0- to 4-point scale as shown in the rubric below. The highest raw score (number of points) a student can achieve on the reading portion of the rest is 39 points.

Rubric for Scoring Open-Ended Reading Questions

Points	Criteria
4	A 4-point response clearly demonstrates understanding of the task, completes all requirements, and provides a clear and focused explanation/opinion that links to or extends aspects of the text.
3	A 3-point response demonstrates an understanding of the task, addresses all requirements, and provides some explanation/opinion using situations or ideas from the text as support.
2	A 2-point response may address all of the requirements, but demonstrates a partial understanding of the task, and uses text incorrectly or with limited success resulting in an inconsistent or flawed explanation.
1	A 1-point response demonstrates minimal understanding of the task, does not address part of the requirements, and provides only a vague reference to or no use of the text.
0	A 0-point response is irrelevant or off-topic.

Compositions on the writing portion of the test are evaluated using a holistic scoring rubric developed specifically to focus on essential features of good writing, including content and organization, usage, sentence construction, and mechanics. Each student's composition is scored on a 1-to-5-point scale, which is a modified version of the New Jersey's Registered Holistic Scoring Rubric. That score is then doubled to yield a maximum possible writing score of 10 points per prompt (20 per test). A copy of the rubric can be found on the New Jersey Department of Education website.

The highest possible raw score on the NJ ASK LAL (reading plus writing) is 59 points. For statistical reasons, student raw scores are converted to scale scores. Scale scores on the NJ ASK range from 100 to 300. Scale scores are used to determine if a student has performed at, below, or above proficiency. Generally speaking, students with a scale score of 200 are performing at the level of "proficient."

NJ ASK *Language* Arts Literacy Standards

*W1 Recognizing a Central Idea or Theme   A central idea or theme is a statement that is broad enough to cover the entire scope of the reading passage. The central idea or theme may be stated or implied, but clues to it are found in the ideas that tend to recur in the text. Examples of a central idea or theme statement include the following:

> **Imagination helps us to solve problems.**

> **Ordinary objects can be used to create unusual art.**

W2   Recognizing Supporting Details   These questions focus on meaningful details that contribute to the development of a character or the plot or that develop ideas and information that are essential to the central idea of a text.

W3   Extrapolating Information, Following Directions   These questions focus on ideas and information implied by, but not explicit in, the text. For example, students may be asked to draw from cues provided in the text in order to identify how a character feels. For everyday texts, students may be asked to infer directions from texts such as recipes or how-to articles.

W4   Paraphrasing, Retelling (Vocabulary)   These questions focus on the meaning of words used in the text and elicit students' use of effective reading strategies to determine the meaning. Targeted vocabulary will always occur within a semantic and syntactic context that students should draw on to respond to the question.

W5   Recognizing Text Organization   Text organization encompasses the patterns of organization that characterize the respective genres. For the narratives, questions focus on setting, character, and plot as well as on any distinctive pattern within the story such as repetition. For everyday texts, questions address structural features such as section topics, charts, and illustrations, in addition to patterns of organization within the text (such as sequence, comparison-contrast, or cause-effect).

W6   Recognizing a Purpose for Reading   These questions, which focus on the reader's purpose, address reasons for reading a particular text. A story, for example, may convey specific information about a species of animal or a culture although that may not be the primary purpose of the text.

---

* Standards with a *W* (for "working with text") focus on ideas and information that are presented in the text and available either literally or by extrapolation.

*A1 Questioning, Clarifying, Predicting   These questions draw on students' use of reading strategies to construct meaning. The questions introduce a focus and a context for responding (e.g., asking a question of the author or a character), and ask students to select and analyze ideas and information from the text to develop a response. Given the nature of this task, these questions are almost always open-ended items.

A2 Predicting Tentative Meanings   These questions focus on statements within the text that introduce some ambiguity: either the ideas are not fully explained or the statement uses language that can be read in two or more ways. For these questions, students use their knowledge of language and of the context within the reading passage to analyze the meaning of a particular statement.

A3 Forming Opinions about Text and Author's Techniques   These questions elicit students' response to aspects of the text. The questions introduce a focus (e.g. whether the main character would make a good friend) and ask students to select and analyze ideas and information from the text to develop a response. Given the nature of this task, opinion questions are always open-ended. Questions on author's techniques elicit the author's viewpoint and techniques used to convey the author's point of view.

A4 Making Judgments, Drawing Conclusions   These questions ask students to draw conclusions based on knowledge they have garnered from the ideas and information within the text. For example, students might be asked to analyze how the setting (e.g., the season of the year) affects the sequence of events within a story, or to analyze the effect of skipping a step in a certain procedure.

A5 Interpreting Literary Elements and Textual Conventions   These questions focus on devices used by the author. Students might be asked to analyze what a specific metaphor conveys about a character in the story, or why an author uses italics for certain words.

* Standards with an *A* (for "analyzing/critiquing text") focus on students' analysis of what they have read.

NJ ASK Language Arts Literacy Standards*

W1	**Recognizing a Central Idea or Theme**	page 3
W2	**Recognizing Supporting Details**	page 3
W3	**Extrapolating Information, Following Directions**	page 35
W4	**Paraphrasing, Retelling (Vocabulary)**	page 19
W5	**Recognizing Text Organization**	pages 35, 51, 81
W6	**Recognizing a Purpose for Reading**	page 51
A1	**Questioning, Clarifying, Predicting**	page 67
A2	**Predicting Tentative Meanings**	page 19, 51
A3	**Forming Opinions about Text and Author's Techniques**	page 67
A4	**Making Judgments, Drawing Conclusions**	page 67
A5	**Interpreting Literary Elements and Textual Conventions**	page 81

* The Standards presented in this book were created by the New Jersey State Department of Education. Source: New Jersey Assessment of Skills and Knowledge, *2009 Score Interpretation Manual, Grades 3–8:* October 2009: Copyright © New Jersey Department of Education. For more information, visit the department's website at http://www.state.nj.us/education/aps/cccs/lal/

Standards with a *W* (for "working with text") focus on ideas and information that are presented in the text and available either literally or by extrapolation. Standards with an *A* (for "analyzing/critiquing text") focus on students' analysis of what they have read.

New Jersey Assessment of Skills and Knowledge

LANGUAGE ARTS LITERACY   Grade 4

Section 1: Reading

Chapter 1

Main Idea and Supporting Details

Clusters

W1 Recognizing a Central Idea or Theme   A central idea or theme is a statement that is broad enough to cover the entire scope of the reading passage. The central idea or theme may be stated or implied, but clues to it are found in the ideas that tend to recur in the text. Examples of a central idea of theme statement include:

Imagination helps us to solve problems.

Ordinary objects can be used to create unusual art.

W2 Recognizing Supporting Details   These questions focus on meaningful details that contribute to the development of a character or the plot, or that develop ideas and information that are essential to the central idea of a text.

Main Idea

In this chapter, you will learn how to find the main idea of a story or article and how to find supporting details. The **main idea** is what a story or article is *mostly* about. Read this paragraph:

Did you know that no two clouds are exactly the same? Even though they are different, clouds are grouped into categories or types. Cirrus clouds form high up in the sky when it is very cold. They look long and feathery. You might see these clouds on a cold winter day. Stratus clouds form low to the ground and usually make the sky look dark and gloomy. Cumulus clouds are large and fluffy. They are easy to see, because, like stratus clouds, they are low to the ground. You are likely to see cumulus clouds on days when the sky is blue.

What is this paragraph mostly about?

(A) cirrus clouds

(B) stratus clouds

(C) cumulus clouds

(D) kinds of clouds

When you choose the main idea, choose the answer choice that tells what the whole passage is about. The entire passage is not about cirrus, stratus, or cumulus clouds. It is about different kinds of clouds. Answer choice D is correct. Answer choices A, B, and C refer to supporting details. **Supporting details** back up, or support, the main idea.

Supporting Details

You just learned that supporting details back up the main idea. They support, or give more information about, the main idea. Using a web like the one shown on the next page can help you find supporting details. Notice that the main idea of the paragraph about clouds is in the center circle. One supporting detail and information about this detail have been added in a circle to help you get started. Add more circles with supporting details from the paragraph about clouds.

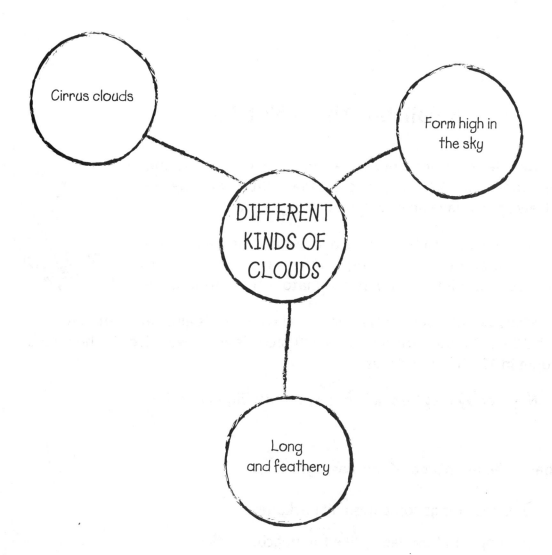

Theme

Fiction, or a made-up story, usually has a theme. The **theme** is the message or lesson in the story. You usually can't put your finger on a sentence stating the theme. You have to look at the supporting details to figure out the theme. (This is sometimes also true with main idea. Sometimes you can't put your finger on a sentence stating the main idea. Sometimes you have to figure it out yourself.) Read this passage about New Jersey.

Practice Passage

Small, But That's Not All

New Jersey is not a big state, but it still has a lot going on. It has more than 120 miles of coastline. That means the people of New Jersey have an easy time getting to the beach.

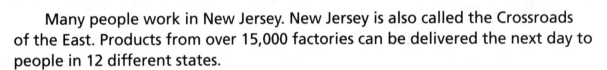

New Jersey is called the Garden State. It has many farms where cranberries, blueberries, peaches, and tomatoes grow. Some people think that a Jersey tomato is the best in the world.

Many people work in New Jersey. New Jersey is also called the Crossroads of the East. Products from over 15,000 factories can be delivered the next day to people in 12 different states.

New Jersey may be small in size, but it's big in activity.

What is the main idea of this passage?

Ⓐ Good things come in small packages.

Ⓑ People in New Jersey like the beach.

Ⓒ New Jersey has the best tomatoes.

Ⓓ Small states can have many factories.

To answer the question you have to think about the author's message in the passage. Is the author saying that New Jersey is small, but good things happen there? This seems to be a good choice because all the details in the passage support this idea. However, read all the answer choices before making a decision. Is the author's message that the people in New Jersey like the beach (answer choice B)? Probably not. This is a supporting detail. The same is true for answer choices C and D. These are supporting details. Answer choice A is the best answer because it gives the main message of the *entire* passage.

Passage 1

Read the story below and on the following page. Then answer the questions about the story. Use the hints underneath each question to help you choose the right answer.

Tanya's Wish

"Tanya? Are you daydreaming again?" asked mom. "You're supposed to be helping me in the kitchen."

Tanya blushed when she realized that her mother was trying to hand her a dish towel. But Tanya was lost in her thoughts.

Ever since she was little, Tanya had loved watching planes fly overhead. Other people wished on stars, but Tanya wished on planes. Whenever one went by she wished "One day I am going to travel on a plane." She thought to herself, "Tanya, you just have to be patient."

Then last week she learned that her wish was about to come true. Her mother said. "How would you like to spend spring break with your cousins in Florida?"

Tanya could hardly believe her ears. Since then, her first plane trip is all she has been thinking about. Tanya was about to get what she had wanted for so long. She just couldn't stop smiling.

Questions

1. **What did Tanya do when she saw a plane?**

   Ⓐ She thought of her cousins.

   Ⓑ She made a wish.

   Ⓒ She took a trip.

   Ⓓ She told her mother.

HINT

This question asks about supporting details. If you aren't sure of the answer, scan the story to see where it talks about what happened when Tanya saw a plane (the third paragraph). Then reread the paragraph to find out what Tanya did.

2.   **What did Tanya's mother want her to do?**

Ⓐ   She wanted Tanya to call her cousins.

Ⓑ   She wanted Tanya to stop making wishes.

Ⓒ   She wanted Tanya to help with the dishes.

Ⓓ   She wanted Tanya to stay at home.

HINT

This question also asks for a supporting detail. If you aren't sure of the answer, scan the story to look for mention of Tanya's mother.

3.   **What is the theme of "Tanya's Wish"?**

Ⓐ   Wishes are only for little children.

Ⓑ   Helping around the house is important.

Ⓒ   Wishes always come true.

Ⓓ   If you are patient, you may get what you want.

HINT

This question asks about the theme, or central idea of the story. What is the big idea in the story? What does Tanya tell herself? What happens at the end of the story?

Passage 2

Read the story below. Then answer the questions about the story. Use the hints underneath each question to help you choose the right answer.

Changing the Sound of Music

Popular music hasn't always sounded the way it does now. For about twenty years, from the 1930s to the 1950s, many people liked to listen to types of music called "jazz" and "swing." One famous piano player, Count Basie, led a band that was one of the most popular to play these types of music. In fact, his band made a certain style of jazz famous because they played it so well.

Count Basie was born August 21, 1904, in Red Bank, New Jersey. His real name was William Basie. William's parents taught him about music. His father played a special type of horn, and his mother played the piano and was his first music teacher. William worked very hard at learning to play the piano and learned to play very well.

In the early 1900s, movies did not have sound, the way that they do today. The movies switched between showing a short scene and then showing the words the characters spoke. Many theaters hired people to play music during the movie so audiences would have something to listen to. William wanted to play for theaters. After a lot of practice, William began to play at the local theater. With more practice, he joined local bands, and one of those bands went on a national tour.

Back then it was difficult to travel, so most bands played in only one city. William played with a band in Kansas City, but this band broke up when William was only twenty-three. William wound up halfway across the country without a way to get home. This actually ended up being a good thing, however.

Alone in Kansas City, William joined another band that stayed around the Midwest. This band traveled a little, and this gave William a chance to listen to how music was played in different regions of the country. When that band fell apart, William formed his own band. William chose people he knew from earlier bands, and the new group began to play in Kansas City. Because the musicians had played with William before, they played well together, and soon the band was on the local radio. Instead of calling William by his real first name, the announcer told listeners they were hearing "Count" Basie and his orchestra. The announcer told William that "Count" made him sound more important as a band leader. The name stuck, the band became popular, and Count Basie decided to take his "orchestra" on the road.

In 1937, William's thirteen-person band played in Chicago before they decided to move on to the big lights of New York City. Count Basie's band sounded different from most bands in New York City. Some people liked their sound, but others did not. But the Count and his band were determined to do well in New York City. They landed a gig in a small New York City club, and it was broadcast on the radio. Then the Count Basie Orchestra began to play regular shows in New York. For the next decade, the band featured famous jazz musicians and worked to keep its special jazz style.

By 1950, the sound of popular music had changed, and Count Basie added different musicians to his band to change its style. Even though the band changed members and its style, famous jazz musicians still wanted to play with Count Basie, who continued to delight listeners with his beautiful music.

As Count Basie grew older, his health worsened. To give him rest, the band had different musicians play the piano in place of Count Basie. Often, these musicians had played with Basie before, when they were all younger. Count Basie still did everything he could to play shows, however, and sometimes he was wheeled onto the stage in a wheelchair. Count Basie loved to have his hands dance across the piano keys and direct the musicians through old tunes like "April in Paris" that had made them famous.

After many years of playing shows, recording albums, and receiving awards, Count Basie passed away in 1984. But his style of music continued on after his death. His friends took over the band, and the group kept on playing. Count Basie helped shape the way jazz music is played today.

Questions

1. **How did Count Basie learn about music in places other than Kansas City?**

    Ⓐ He asked friends who lived in Kansas City to visit local clubs.

    Ⓑ He joined a band that traveled to other nearby areas.

    Ⓒ He spent a lot of time listening to the radio to learn about styles.

    Ⓓ He traveled to New York and to other places in the country.

 HINT

> This question is about a supporting detail. Read the selection again, and pay attention to how he first reached the Midwest.

2. **Who gave Count Basie the name "Count"?**

Ⓐ his parents

Ⓑ a bandleader

Ⓒ his drummer

Ⓓ an announcer

HINT

This question also looks for a supporting detail. If you do not know the answer, reread the passage, and pay careful attention to wherever you see the word "Count."

3. **What is this story mostly about?**

Ⓐ the famous bandleader Count Basie

Ⓑ the history of jazz and swing music

Ⓒ famous singers who sang with bands

Ⓓ how jazz music changed over the years

HINT

What does most of the article discuss? Think about whether it mainly discusses a person's life or a type of music.

Passage 3

Read the story below. Then answer the questions about the story. Use the hints underneath each question to help you choose the right answer.

Annie and the School Shopper

A modern-day fable based on Aesop's "The Ant and the Grasshopper"

Annie loved summer. She enjoyed lying about in the grass, looking up at the puffy clouds, dipping her toes in the pool, and singing songs to herself. She was happy to not be in school, where it seemed she could never quite keep up. She was always flipping through her messy notebook pages and missing what the teacher said, or daydreaming about reading books while not really paying attention to them at all.

One day as Annie spread out her towel and prepared to enjoy the sunny summer, she saw her neighbor Susan getting out of her parents' car with a bunch of shopping bags. Susan was the same age as Annie and they attended the same school. They were even in the same class. Annie wondered whether Susan had bought new clothes for school. After Susan went inside, Annie decided to run over to her house to see what Susan had bought.

Susan welcomed her by asking, "Want to see what I bought?" Susan showed Annie notebooks. Surprised, Annie rifled through the shopping bag, looking for something fun, but all she found were pens and pencils, notebooks and paper, a dictionary and a thesaurus. When Annie looked up, she was surprised to see Susan staring at her proudly as if she were having the best day ever.

"That's great, Susan," Annie said, but she really didn't mean it. "Maybe when you finish putting all your new stuff away, you can come over and hang by the pool with me." Annie pointed to her backyard, where the sun seemed to be shining directly onto her towel. The pool sparkled invitingly.

"No, thanks," Susan said. "I'd rather go inside and open all of my new supplies. I think I'll write my name in my new notebooks. I might even start reading my English textbook. It looks like we'll be reading some mystery stories by Marley Abbot this year!"

Annie rolled her eyes over to her own backyard. There was still at least a week until school started, and Annie was in no hurry for classes to begin. "Why bother with school stuff? Who needs books and pens in the summer?" Annie made her way back to poolside, where she lay back on her towel and enjoyed the warm sunshine.

During the next week, Annie and Susan continued their usual pastimes. Annie spent her remaining days by the pool, while Susan spent her time getting ready for class.

On the first day of fourth grade, Susan and Annie waited at the bus stop together. They went into class together, and they even sat next to each other. As English class started, the teacher said, "This year we will be reading the stories of Marley Abbot. Can anyone tell the class anything about Marley Abbot?"

Susan's hand shot up immediately. Annie could see that she was excited to share what she had learned. Annie yawned while Susan listed interesting facts about the writer and his work. Annie would have liked to have copied the information down, but she had no pencil and no paper.

Questions

1. **What is a theme of "Annie and the School Shopper"?**

   Ⓐ School can be very hard.

   Ⓑ Reading can be great fun.

   Ⓒ It is good to be prepared.

   Ⓓ Kids should enjoy the summer.

   HINT

   What message is the author trying to get across to readers? Think about why it's better to be like Susan.

2. **What was in Susan's bags?**

   Ⓐ library books

   Ⓑ a towel and sunscreen

   Ⓒ school supplies

   Ⓓ new school clothes

   HINT

   This question is about a supporting detail. You can find the answer right in the passage.

3. **What does Annie do while Susan gets ready for school?**

    Ⓐ buy school supplies

    Ⓑ talk about Marley Abbot

    Ⓒ lie in the sun by the pool

    Ⓓ read mystery stories

HINT

You can find a clue to the answer of this question in the first paragraph.

4. **What is the first paragraph of this story mostly about?**

    Ⓐ how Susan gets ready for school

    Ⓑ why Annie likes the summer

    Ⓒ why Annie sings songs

    Ⓓ what Annie does in school

HINT

Reread the first paragraph. Separate the main idea from the supporting details.

Chapter 2

Understanding New Words

Clusters

W4   Paraphrasing/Retelling (Vocabulary)   These questions focus on the meaning of words used in the text and elicit students' use of effective reading strategies to determine the meaning. Targeted vocabulary will always occur within a semantic and syntactic context that students should draw on to respond to the question.

A2   Predicting Tentative Meanings   These questions focus on statements within the text that introduce some ambiguity; either the ideas are not fully explained or the statement uses language that can be read in two or more ways. For these questions, students use their knowledge of language and of the context within the reading passage to analyze the meaning of a particular statement.

New Words

What do you do when you are reading and come across a new word? Do you look up the word in a dictionary or skip over the new word and keep on reading? If you're like most people, you probably try to figure out the meaning of the new word by looking at the words around it. This is called looking for **context clues**. On the New Jersey ASK, you may be asked to choose the meaning of some words that are new to you. You can usually figure out the meaning of these words by looking at the context clues.

Read this sentence:

For gym class, girls with long hair must tie it back using a <u>thingie-wigger</u>.

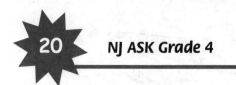

"Thingie-wigger" is not a real word. However, you can tell from the context that it is some kind of hair tie.

Let's try another one:

> **To play <u>bicky-diddle</u>, you line up a ball on a tee and hit it with a small stick.**

What do you think "bicky-diddle" is? It's a kind of game, for sure. The context clues—a ball, a tee, and a small stick—help you reach this conclusion.

Now you try it.

> **Half-asleep, Christina made her way toward the kitchen. Her eyes were opened only halfway, and her arms and legs ached. Even though it was 10 A.M., Christina felt really <u>sluggish</u> and wished she could go back to bed.**

What do you think the word "sluggish" means?

_____

What context clues helped you reach this conclusion?

_____

Words with More Than One Meaning

Some words have more than one meaning, which can make it even harder to figure out their correct meaning. Always look at the context, the words and sentences around the word, before choosing an answer. The following sentences contain words with more than one meaning:

> **Please turn off the <u>light</u> when you leave the room.**

> **A feather is very <u>light</u> and can float in the air.**

What does the word "light" mean in the first sentence?

_____

What does it mean in the second sentence?

_____

Now read these sentences.

The casserole will stay fresh if you cover it with <u>foil</u> and put it in the refrigerator.

The police <u>foiled</u> the robber's attempt to steal money from the safe.

What does the word "foil" mean in the first sentence?

_____

What does it mean in the second sentence?

_____

Practice Passage

Now read this passage and answer the question.

New Jersey's State Bird

New Jersey named the American Goldfinch as the state bird in 1935. This bird is also called a wild canary. It is petite and grows only to about five inches long. It is brightly-colored in yellow, black, and white. The American Goldfinch mostly eats seeds.

This little bird likes to live in trees where it can find seeds. You will see it in the spring and summer in New Jersey. In the winter, goldfinches gather in large flocks and fly to warm places in the south.

What does the word "petite" mean in the first paragraph of the passage?

Ⓐ colorful

Ⓑ tiny

Ⓒ wild

Ⓓ warm

You can figure out the meaning of the word "petite" by looking at the context clues. The phrase "grows only to about 5 inches" should give you a clue. Is that a big bird or a small bird? It's quite small. The second paragraph also says that the bird is little. You can tell from the context of the passage that the bird is small. "Petite" means small. Answer choice B is the best answer.

Passage 1

Read the story below. Then answer the questions about the story. Use the hints underneath each question to help you choose the right answer.

Max Has a Dream

"I had the weirdest dream last night," Max said rubbing his eyes.

"What happened?" asked his brother Mike.

"I dreamt I was sailing in a boat. I sailed to an island. When I got off the boat, there was no one on the island. It was deserted, and I was all alone."

"What happened next?" asked Mike.

"I looked around. I was cautious, and I took my time. I was afraid someone might be lurking behind a tree."

"Did you find anyone?" asked Mike.

"I sure did," Max said smiling. "You were on the island too!"

Questions

1. **What does the word "deserted" mean in this sentence from the story: "It was deserted, and I was all alone."?**

    Ⓐ noisy

    Ⓑ scary

    Ⓒ empty

    Ⓓ busy

HINT

Look at the context clues in this sentence and in other sentences in the paragraph. Did Max see anyone else at first?

2. **What does the word "cautious" mean in the fifth paragraph of the story?**

    Ⓐ wild

    Ⓑ careful

    Ⓒ confused

    Ⓓ relaxed

HINT

Reread the fifth paragraph. How was Max behaving?

Passage 2

Read the newsletter on page 27. Then answer the questions about the newsletter. Use the hints underneath each question to help you choose the right answer.

FARMING FOREVER

HAYRIDES...
It's that time of year again!

Nothing makes you appreciate the beauty of autumn more than a hayride through the pumpkin patch at Shamrock Farms. Bring the whole family—and dress warmly!

Warm apple cider and homemade pumpkin bread will be waiting for you upon your return!

Purchase your tickets in advance by calling: 555-FARM

Where:
Shamrock Farms
217 Dairy Barn Rd.
Anywhere, NJ

When:
Oct. 15 – Nov. 15
6 p.m. – midnight*

Cost:
Adults $5.00
Children $3.00

Last hayride leaves at 11:30 p.m.

BETTER BUTTER

By Camilla Turso

Farm-fresh butter is a real treat, and the folks at First Prize Dairy Farm are giving it away for free—to kids, that is! John Colbert, owner and operator of First Prize Dairy Farm, has recently opened his farm to school field trips. The field trip includes tours of the dairy barn and the building where they make First Prize Dairy's award-winning ice cream. For kids, the highlight of the trip is a sampling of homemade bread and butter.

"Each day, I make a new batch of butter and several loaves of homemade bread," said Margaret Colbert, John's wife. "The kids seem to love having the little snack before they hop back on their school buses."

And just how is this butter made? Each day, Margaret gets milk from a few of the cows. She sets this milk aside until it gets a little bit sour. After a while, the cream from the milk floats to the top. She scoops this cream off the top and places it in a special jar. Inside the jar is a paddle turned by a handle. Margaret turns the handle until the fat from the cream collects on the paddle.

This fat is what she uses to make the butter. The liquid that's left behind is called buttermilk. Margaret sometimes uses the buttermilk for baking. "Once the butter has separated from the cream, I remove it and place it in a bowl," said Margaret.

Then Margaret presses on the butter to push out any remaining buttermilk. Next, she rinses the butter with cold water. She continues pressing on the butter until the water is no longer cloudy.

"When it's done, I sprinkle in just a pinch or two of salt for flavor," said Margaret. "Then it's ready to serve."

If you would like to try some of Margaret's delicious, farm-fresh butter, it will be on sale for a limited time at the First Prize Dairy.

Questions? Comments?
Contact us:
Farming Forever , c/o Shannon Gilbert, Editor
123 Pine Mill Rd., Anywhere, NJ 01234
(555) 555-4EVR

❓ Questions ❓

1. **What does the word "appreciate" mean in the following sentence: "Nothing makes you appreciate the beauty of autumn more than a hayride through the pumpkin patch at Shamrock Farms"?**

    Ⓐ look for

    Ⓑ have fun

    Ⓒ be glad about

    Ⓓ see up close

HINT

Cross out answer choices that you know are wrong. Then choose the best answer.

2. **What does the word "separated" mean in the following sentence: "Once the butter has separated from the cream, I remove it and place it in a bowl"?**

    Ⓐ part of

    Ⓑ mixed into

    Ⓒ disappeared

    Ⓓ moved away from

HINT

Remember that the butter is able to be removed and placed in a bowl.

3. **What does the word "pinch" mean in the second-to-last paragraph of "Better Butter"?**

    Ⓐ grab

    Ⓑ little bit

    Ⓒ press

    Ⓓ cupful

HINT

Read the sentence carefully. The word "pinch" has more than one meaning. Choose the answer choice that tells what the word means in this sentence.

Passage 3

Read the story below. Then answer the questions about the story. Use the hints underneath each question to help you choose the right answer.

Excerpt from *The Wonderful Wizard of Oz*

by L. Frank Baum

When Dorothy awoke the sun was shining through the trees and Toto had long been out chasing birds and squirrels around him. She sat up and looked around her. Scarecrow was still standing patiently in his corner, waiting for her.

"We must go and search for water," she said to him.

"Why do you want water?" he asked.

"To wash my face clean after the dust of the road, and to drink, so the dry bread will not stick in my throat."

"It must be inconvenient to be made of flesh," said the Scarecrow thoughtfully, "for you must sleep, and eat and drink. However, you have brains, and it is worth a lot of bother to be able to think properly."

They left the cottage and walked through the trees until they found a little spring of clear water, where Dorothy drank and bathed and ate her breakfast. She saw there was not much bread left in the basket, and the girl was thankful the Scarecrow did not have to eat anything, for there was scarcely enough for herself and Toto for the day.

When she had finished her meal, and was about to go back to the road of yellow brick, she was startled to hear a deep groan nearby.

"What was that?" she asked timidly.

"I cannot imagine," replied the Scarecrow; "but we can go and see."

Just then another groan reached their ears, and the sound seemed to come from behind them. They turned and walked through the forest a few steps, when Dorothy discovered something shining in a ray of sunshine that fell between the trees. She ran to the place and then stopped short, with a little cry of surprise.

One of the big trees had been partly chopped through, and standing beside it, with an uplifted axe in his hands, was a man made entirely of tin. His head and arms and legs were jointed upon his body, but he stood perfectly motionless, as if he could not stir at all.

Dorothy looked at him in amazement, and so did the Scarecrow, while Toto barked sharply and made a snap at the tin legs, which hurt his teeth.

"Did you groan?" asked Dorothy.

"Yes," answered the tin man, "I did. I've been groaning for more than a year, and no one has ever heard me before or come to help me."

"What can I do for you?" she inquired softly, for she was moved by the sad voice in which the man spoke.

"Get an oil-can and oil my joints," he answered. "They are rusted so badly that I cannot move them at all; if I am well oiled I shall soon be all right again. You will find an oil-can on a shelf in my cottage."

Dorothy at once ran back to the cottage and found the oil-can, and then she returned and asked anxiously, "Where are your joints?"

"Oil my neck, first," replied the Tin Woodman. So she oiled it, and as it was quite badly rusted the Scarecrow took hold of the tin head and moved it gently from side to side until it worked freely, and then the man could turn it himself.

"Now oil the joints in my arms," he said. And Dorothy oiled them and the Scarecrow bent them carefully until they were quite free from rust and as good as new.

The Tin Woodman gave a sigh of satisfaction and lowered his axe, which he leaned against the tree.

"This is a great comfort," he said. "I have been holding that axe in the air ever since I rusted, and I'm glad to be able to put it down at last. Now, if you will oil the joints of my legs, I shall be all right once more."

So they oiled his legs until he could move them freely; and he thanked them again and again for his release, for he seemed a very polite creature, and very grateful.

"I might have stood there always if you had not come along," he said; "so you have certainly saved my life. How did you happen to be here?"

"We are on our way to the Emerald City to see the Great Oz," she answered, "and we stopped at your cottage to pass the night."

"Why do you wish to see Oz?" he asked.

"I want him to send me back to Kansas, and the Scarecrow wants him to put a few brains into his head," she replied.

The Tin Woodman appeared to think deeply for a moment. Then he said:

"Do you suppose Oz could give me a heart?"

"Why, I guess so," Dorothy answered. "It would be as easy as to give the Scarecrow brains."

"True," the Tin Woodman returned. "So, if you will allow me to join your party, I will also go to the Emerald City and ask Oz to help me."

"Come along," said the Scarecrow heartily, and Dorothy added that she would be pleased to have his company. So the Tin Woodman shouldered his axe and they all passed through the forest until they came to the road that was paved with yellow brick.

The Tin Woodman had asked Dorothy to put the oil-can in her basket. "For," he said, "if I should get caught in the rain, and rust again, I would need the oil-can badly."

It was a bit of good luck to have their new comrade join the party, for soon after they had begun their journey again they came to a place where the trees and branches grew so thick over the road that the travelers could not pass. But the Tin Woodman set to work with his axe and chopped so well that soon he cleared a passage for the entire party.

Dorothy was thinking so earnestly as they walked along that she did not notice when the Scarecrow stumbled into a hole and rolled over to the side of the road. Indeed he was obliged to call to her to help him up again.

"Why didn't you walk around the hole?" asked the Tin Woodman.

"I don't know enough," replied the Scarecrow cheerfully. "My head is stuffed with straw, you know, and that is why I am going to Oz to ask him for some brains."

"Oh, I see," said the Tin Woodman. "But, after all, brains are not the best things in the world."

"Have you any?" inquired the Scarecrow.

"No, my head is quite empty," answered the Woodman. "But once I had brains, and a heart also; so, having tried them both, I should much rather have a heart."

"And why is that?" asked the Scarecrow.

"I will tell you my story, and then you will know."

Questions

1. What does the word "motionless" mean in the following sentence: "His head and arms and legs were jointed upon his body, but he stood perfectly motionless, as if he could not stir at all"?

   (A) in motion

   (B) little motion

   (C) without motion

   (D) hoping for motion

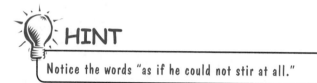

HINT

Notice the words "as if he could not stir at all."

2. What does the word "comrade" mean in the following sentence: "It was a bit of good luck to have their new comrade join the party, for soon after they had begun their journey again they came to a place where the trees and branches grew so thick over the road that the travelers could not pass."

   (A) axe

   (B) oil-can

   (C) girl

   (D) friend

HINT

The "comrade" is the Tin Woodman.

3. What does the word "earnestly" mean in the following sentence: "Dorothy was thinking so earnestly as they walked along that she did not notice when the Scarecrow stumbled into a hole and rolled over to the side of the road"?

   Ⓐ deeply

   Ⓑ sadly

   Ⓒ clearly

   Ⓓ differently

   HINT

   Remember that Dorothy did not even notice when Scarecrow fell into a hole.

4. What does the word "inquired" mean at the end of the story?

   Ⓐ asked

   Ⓑ said

   Ⓒ ordered

   Ⓓ shouted

   HINT

   The sentence containing the word has a question mark after it.

Chapter 3

Following Directions

Clusters

W3   Extrapolating Information, Following Directions   These questions focus on ideas and information implied by, but not explicit in, the text. For everyday texts, students may be asked to infer directions from texts such as recipes or how-to articles.

W5   Recognizing Text Organization   Text organization encompasses the patterns of organization that characterize the respective genres. For everyday texts, questions address structural features such as section topics, charts, and illustrations, in addition to patterns of organization within the text (such as sequence, comparison-contrast, or cause-effect).

Introduction

The everyday texts on the New Jersey ASK are the kind of writing you might see in daily life. An everyday text might be a magazine or newspaper article or a how-to article, which is an article with steps or directions. You will often have to follow directions in an everyday text. These passages may have steps in them and may have headings such as Step 1 and Step 2 or just numbers before the steps. These passages might also have pictures showing you how to do something. A recipe is a kind of everyday text. Read the following recipe:

Practice Passage

How to Make Fresh Fruit-sicles

Want a yummy treat that will keep you cool in the summer? Try these fresh fruit-sicles, which you can make yourself.

Here is what you will need:

1 cup of watermelon pieces (make sure to take out the seeds)

1 cup of orange juice

1 cup of water

an ice cube tray

foil

toothpicks

Step 1. Mix your fruit.

Mix together your watermelon pieces, orange juice, and water in a large bowl. Make sure you mash up the watermelon until your mixture is smooth.

Step 2. Pour your fruity mixture.

Next, carefully pour your mixture into the ice cube tray until each area in the tray is filled. Be careful not to fill the ice cube tray too much!

Step 3. Cover it up.

After pouring your mixture, cover the ice cube tray with foil. Be careful with this step. You don't want to spill any of the fruity mixture.

Step 4. Put a stick in it.

Now stick a toothpick into each separate area of the ice cube tray.

Step 5. Freeze it.

Put the ice cube tray into the freezer for a few hours. Don't move the ice cube tray around too much, or the fresh fruit-sicles will not set.

Step 6. Enjoy!

Once the fresh fruit-sicles are frozen, gently pull the foil off of the ice-cube tray. Try not to break any of the toothpicks. Crack the fresh fruit-sicles out of the tray just as you would regular ice cubes. Pick one up and enjoy the icy snack you can make yourself!

Questions

1. **The purpose of the first step is to**

    Ⓐ tell you how to make a mixture smooth.

    Ⓑ teach you how to stay cool in the summer.

    Ⓒ teach you how to mix fruit together.

    Ⓓ tell you to mix the fruit together.

Reread the first step to answer this question. The author includes this step to tell you to do something. While the author tells you to mash up the watermelon until your mixture is smooth, the author doesn't really tell you how to do this, so answer choice A is probably not the best answer. Step 1 doesn't teach you how to stay cool in the summer (answer choice B). It also doesn't teach you how to mix fruit together (answer choice C), but it does tell you to mix the fruit together (answer choice D). Answer choice D is the best answer.

2. **What is the purpose of the ice cube tray? Write your answer on the line below.**

    _____

You can tell from the recipe that the ice cube tray shapes the liquid until it freezes. It makes the fruit-sicles small and easy to eat.

Passage 1

Read this passage and answer the questions that follow. Use the hint below each question to help you choose the correct answer.

Any Way the Wind Blows

Today we have many computers and machines that help us figure out what the weather will be like from one day to another. But before such detailed machines were invented, people used basic tools to help them plan for whatever the weather might bring. Wind vanes, which tell us what direction the wind is coming from, are just one example of such tools. These simple instruments have been used for thousands of years, and it is believed that they have been around since the time of the ancient Greeks. Wind vanes help us in many different ways. They are used by pilots as they plot the course of their flights and can help us judge which direction an approaching storm will come from. Weather stations use wind vanes that are hooked up to computers, which instantly record important information. The following directions tell you how to make your own working wind vane.

You Will Need

A small piece of poster board

A pair of scissors

A new pencil

An eraser

A drinking straw

A marker

A straight pin

Procedure

1. Before you start working on your wind vane, ask an adult for help. Because you will be using a pin, which can be sharp, it is important that you get an adult to help you.

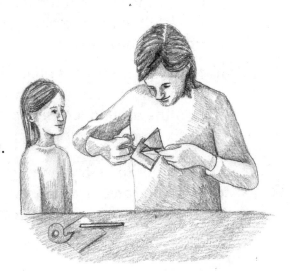

2. Draw a small triangle on the poster board, and then use the scissors to cut out the triangle.

3. Once this triangle is cut out, use it to trace another triangle on the poster board. This will help you to be certain that the two triangles are the exact same size.

4. Once you have done this, cut out the second triangle. These two triangles will be used to make the tail of your wind vane.

5. Place one of the triangles on a flat surface and put the straw on top of the triangle. Make sure that the end of the straw is meeting the flat edge of the triangle. Using the clear tape, secure the straw to the triangle.

6. Place the second triangle on top of the straw and tape the two triangles together, making sure that all three sides of the triangles are taped.

7. Once the straw and the triangles are taped together, balance the straw on your finger. This part might be a little tricky, so you may want the adult to help you with this. Once you find the place where the straw is perfectly balanced on your finger, ask the adult to mark the spot on the straw.

8. Hold the straw so that the edges of the triangle are pointing up and down. Have the adult stick the pin through the place you have marked on the straw so that it pokes through.

9. Have the adult push the pin into the eraser of the new pencil. Make sure that the straw spins smoothly around on the end of the eraser. If it does not, have the adult adjust the pin so that it moves smoothly around the tip of the pencil.

10. Now you are ready to take your wind vane outside. You can push the straw into the ground, or use a piece of clay to fix it to a porch or railing.

Ask the adult to help you find north, using a compass. Once you know where north is, you can use your wind vane to see which way the wind is blowing. Your wind vane will point into the direction that the wind is coming from.

Questions

1. **The purpose of the first paragraph is to**

   Ⓐ give the reader information about weather stations.

   Ⓑ explain to the reader what wind vanes are used for.

   Ⓒ show the reader where to purchase a wind vane.

   Ⓓ tell the reader who invented the first wind vane.

HINT

Reread the first paragraph. What information is the author trying to give the reader in this paragraph?

2. **According to the passage, what should you do if the straw does not spin smoothly on top of the pencil?**

    Ⓐ Ask the adult to adjust the pin.

    Ⓑ Find another pencil to use.

    Ⓒ Take the wind vane outside.

    Ⓓ Find another adult to help you.

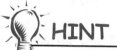HINT

If you are unsure about the answer, reread step 9. You will find the answer to the question in this step.

3. **Explain the purpose of the last paragraph in this passage. Write your answer on the lines below.**

    _____

    _____

    _____

    _____

    _____

Passage 2

Read this passage and answer the questions that follow. Use the hint below each question to help you choose the correct answer.

Play Time

Have you ever been in a school play? Have you ever thought about planning your own play? Planning and performing a play is a lot of fun, especially if you get your friends to help you. The following tips will give you several ideas to help you plan and perform a play.

Decide on a story. The first thing you should do when planning a play is to choose the story that you want to tell. For your first play, you will have a lot of details to think about, so you might want to choose a story that you already know, such as "Little Red Riding Hood," "Snow White," or "Goldilocks and the Three Bears." If you have a good imagination, you can always try writing your own play. However, remember that writing a whole play takes time. Make sure you start writing early enough that you still have time to learn your lines and practice before opening night.

Find a place to perform the play. When deciding where to perform your play, think about the story's setting. If most of the story takes place in a field or in the woods, you should consider performing the play outside. Use the trees and bushes in your yard as props. If you are worried about rain or snow ruining your play, it might be a good idea to set the stage for your play inside. Maybe you have room in your family's garage or basement to set up a stage.

You can transform just about any location by building scenery. This might sound difficult, but you don't need wood and nails to build scenery. A few cardboard boxes will do. Boxes from refrigerators, stoves, washing machines, and dryers work well, because they are very large. Get an adult to help you cut the boxes apart, and then use paint, crayons, or markers to color them in. Use your imagination to make a rainbow-filled sky, a busy city street, or a barn filled with animals.

Choose your role. The next step in planning your play is to choose your role. Perhaps you want to act as a character in the play, or maybe you would rather serve as the director of the play and let your friends do the acting. Either way, you should make a list of all the roles that need to be filled. This will help you determine the number of people you need to perform the play. It's always a good idea to have a few extra people, too. These people are called "understudies." When an actor or actress gets sick, an understudy takes that person's place in the play.

Dress the part. Once you and your friends have chosen your roles, you should make costumes to dress the part. It's not necessary to go out and buy costumes, because you can use your own clothes and ordinary household items to make them. For example, to play the role of Little Red Riding Hood, all you need is a red hooded sweatshirt or jacket. If you don't have one, borrow one from a friend. To play the wolf, pull on some gray socks and mittens to make paws, and paint a few whiskers on your face. Use paper plates, paper bags, or pieces of cardboard to make masks. Ask a parent or guardian to dig some old clothes out of the attic or basement. The more you use your imagination, the better your costumes will be.

Practice your play. Before you perform your play for an audience, you should practice several times. Study your lines carefully so you know what to say and when to say it. Figure out where you need to stand and when you need to enter and exit the stage. Remember, the more you practice, the better your play will be when you finally perform it for a live audience.

Invite friends and family. Let your friends and family know when and where you plan to perform the play for them. Give them plenty of notice so they are sure to attend. If you want, you can give them invitations or tickets to remind them of the date and time of the play.

Have a good time. The most important thing to remember when you are performing your play is to have a good time. It's normal to feel a little bit anxious when performing in front of a crowd. Even people who perform all the time get nervous once in a while. Just remember that the people in the audience are there to see you because they love you and support you. They won't mind even if you forget a few of your lines.

Also, don't worry if something goes wrong. Accidents happen, and there's nothing you can do to stop them. If the scenery tips over, just pretend that it's still standing, or pause for a moment to pick it up. If part of your costume rips, just ignore it. If you trip and fall, get up and keep saying your lines. These

things happen to people all the time, and if anything, they just make your play seem more realistic.

Hand out refreshments. Once the play has ended and you've taken your final bow, be sure to thank your audience for coming. You might even want to invite them to have refreshments such as lemonade and cookies after the show. They will most likely take you up on your offer. After all, who wouldn't want to share cookies with the star of a play?

⁇ Questions ⁇

1. **The purpose of the words in dark print is to**

   Ⓐ give the definitions of difficult words in the article.

   Ⓑ show the most important tips given in the article.

   Ⓒ explain how to become the director of a play.

   Ⓓ explain how to write your own play from scratch.

HINT

Reread the words in dark print. Think about how these words help to divide the article.

2. **In the article, the author states that you should simply have a good time when performing a play. Why does she say this?**

   Ⓐ She thinks that plays are silly.

   Ⓑ She wants you to stay relaxed.

   Ⓒ She has performed in many plays.

   Ⓓ She often forgets a few of her lines.

HINT

Reread the part of the article that says "Have a good time."

3. Explain the reason why it's a good idea to have understudies when you are planning a play. Use information from the article to support your response.

Write your answer on the lines below.

_____

_____

_____

_____

_____

_____

_____

_____

_____

_____

_____

_____

 HINT

Consider what an understudy does. Why is this an important job?

Passage 3

Read the following passage and answer the questions that follow. Use the hint below each question to help you choose the correct answer.

Inventing Ideas

Let's imagine that your teacher asks you to write a story. What should you write about? You need a good idea, or topic, that will make your story fun and interesting—or even amazing and astonishing! Finding just the right topic can be a very difficult task.

You shouldn't use a topic that you think is boring. If you pick a boring topic, you won't enjoy writing the story, and other people may not want to read it. You also don't want a topic that is too large to write about in just one story, or too small to fill up the story. And you probably don't want to write about something you've already written about, or something all your friends are writing about.

To write the best story you can, you should think of an original topic. Find something that nobody else has thought of, that will surprise people and make them want to read. You'll find that a good topic will make writing easier, also. If you feel amused by your topic, or excited by it, you'll be eager to write down your ideas about it.

But how do you find your great new idea? You have to invent it! You may not know it, but there are many fun ways to get your mind working and invent the perfect idea for your story. Here are just a few exercises you can try:

Exercise 1: Pictures Tell a Thousand Words

There's an old saying, "A picture is worth a thousand words." That means that every picture—whether it's a photograph, a simple drawing, or a great painting— tells a story. You can prove that this old saying is true, and it's as easy as looking at pictures. You can use illustrations from books, sketches by your friends, photographs of your family, pictures from a newspaper, books of famous art, or any other pictures.

Finding the pictures can be a lot of fun, but the real fun is the next step. Put the picture you chose in front of you and look at it carefully. Ask yourself some questions about the picture: What is the subject of the picture, and what is the subject doing? What kind of picture is it, and who created the picture?

Use your imagination in asking—and generating answers to—these questions. You'll find that thinking about the picture is challenging your brain to work harder. As you look at the picture, you may discover that a brand-new story is building in your mind!

Exercise 2: Put on Your Thinking Cap

This exercise is also a lot of fun, and it can give you even more great ideas. Here is what you'll need:

1. *old newspapers*

2. *old magazines*

3. *two hats*

4. *a pen and paper*

NOTE: Be sure that nobody else wants to use the magazines and newspapers!

Once you've gathered your materials, it's time for the fun part. You can start ripping and cutting up the newspapers and magazines! Look through the magazines and cut out all of the pictures you think are interesting. Then flip through the newspaper pages and cut out the headlines that catch your attention.

After you've cut out many pictures and headlines, place the headlines inside one hat and the pictures inside another, and mix them all up. You now have a real "thinking cap"—an instant idea machine! To get a unique idea, just reach into the "picture" hat and pull out one picture, and then reach into the "headline" hat and take one headline. Now compare the picture and the headline you chose. Do they match at all, or are they completely different? If you put them together, what kind of stories could you make from them?

This is a good way to think of wild and silly ideas for stories. You might end up with a photograph of a firefighter with a headline about a pie-eating contest, or a picture of a tiger with a headline about a new kind of airplane!

 Questions

1. **The purpose of the "NOTE" in the passage is to**

   (A) make sure the reader skips part of the passage.

   (B) tell the reader what materials are needed.

   (C) add information the reader should know.

   (D) show the reader how to make a "thinking cap."

   HINT

   Find the "NOTE" in the passage. Look at what the note tells you, and what happens before and after the note.

2. **According to Exercise 1, what should you do to make a story out of a painting?**

   (A) Learn exactly what is happening in the painting.

   (B) Ask yourself questions about the painting.

   (C) Find out if the painting can be seen in a museum.

   (D) Ask your teachers whether they have ever seen the painting.

    **HINT**

   Look at Exercise 1 in this passage. It will tell you how to make a story by looking at a painting.

3. **This passage gives two exercises for thinking of new story ideas:**

-   Explain how each of these exercises might be helpful.
-   Decide which one you prefer and explain why.

Use information from the passage to support your response.

_____

_____

_____

_____

_____

_____

_____

_____

_____

_____

_____

HINT

To answer this question, think about what you learned in this passage. Tell about each of the two exercises in the passage. Then tell which one you think would work better for you.

Chapter 4

Author's Purpose and Prediction

Clusters

W6 Recognizing a Purpose for Reading   These questions, which focus on the reader's purpose, address reasons for a particular text. A story, for example, may convey specific information about a species of animal or a culture, although that may not be the primary purpose of the text.

W5 Recognizing Text Organization   Text organization encompasses the patterns of organization that characterize the respective genres. For everyday texts, questions address structural features such as section topics, charts, and illustrations, in addition to patterns of organization within the text (such as sequence, comparison-contrast, or cause-effect).

A2 Predicting Tentative Meanings   These questions focus on statements within the text that introduce some ambiguity: either the ideas are not fully explained or the statement uses language that can be read in two or more ways. For these questions, students use their knowledge of language and of the context within the reading passage to analyze the meaning of a particular statement.

Introduction

Writers write for a reason. Think about the last time you wrote something. Maybe you wrote a short story just for fun, or maybe you wrote a journal entry for English class. Perhaps you wrote down directions to help a friend find your house. Some of the questions on the NJ ASK will ask you why an author wrote a passage.

Have you ever read a book or watched a movie and guessed the ending? Sometimes it's helpful to predict what will happen next when you are reading. Some test questions will ask you what will probably happen next.

Author's Purpose

Authors often write for these reasons:

- To make or convince you to do something

- To describe what something is like

- To entertain with a story about characters

- To inform you about something

- To teach you how to do something

Imagine you wrote your mayor a letter asking for help fixing up a park. The purpose of your letter would be to convince the mayor that this is important. Now imagine you wrote your friend a letter to tell what it is like at your grandmother's house. Your purpose then would be to describe. If you wrote a story for fun, your purpose would be to entertain. If you wrote a report about dolphins at the New Jersey State Aquarium, your purpose would be to inform. If you wrote down the steps your friend should take to get from her house to yours, you would be teaching your friend how to do something.

Write the purpose for each of the following on the line below it.

1. **A letter to an editor trying to get people to help clean up a park**

   _____

2. **A pamphlet telling how to plant a garden**

   _____

3. **A story about a dog that talks to its owner**

   _____

4.   **An article about a new fire truck in your town**

_____

5.   **A story telling what it is like to fly in an airplane**

_____

6.   **A book on the history of trains**

_____

Prediction

When you're reading a book, do you like to guess what will happen next? Most people do. When you make a guess, you're making a **prediction**. On the NJ ASK, you might also be asked to predict in a different way. You might have to predict—or guess—what an author means. For example, imagine an author writes, "Keep the plant in a warm place." How warm is warm? Does the author mean to keep the plant on top of a hot stove? Probably not. The author probably means to keep the plant in a sunny spot in your house that's not cold.

Practice Passage

Read this story and then answer the questions.

The Spelling Bee

Angela stood nervously on the school's stage. She was in the final round of the school spelling bee. She had been studying for the spelling bee for weeks. Her mom and dad had been helping her practice every night. She knew every word from "ability" to "zone." She felt prepared for the contest, but she was still worried that she would be asked to spell a word she did not know.

Suddenly, Angela's teacher asked her to step forward. Then her teacher asked her to spell the word "foreign." Angela felt flushed. She knew the word. She had spelled it a million times, but she couldn't picture it in her mind at the moment. Did the "i" come before the "e"? She couldn't be sure. She knew that there was a rule to remembering which came first, but she couldn't think of it. Angela's teacher asked her to spell the word again. Slowly, Angela started to spell the word. . . .

What do you think will happen next? Write your answer on the lines below.

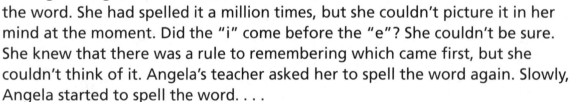

_____

_____

_____

_____

_____

Passage 1

Read this passage and answer the questions that follow. Use the hints below each question to help you choose the correct answer.

The Wonders of Breakfast

Why Eat Breakfast?

1   You've probably heard someone say that breakfast is the most important meal of the day. Well, believe it or not, that's true! Although you think that you're not doing much of anything while you're sleeping all night long, your body is using up the power from the food you ate for dinner.

2   Think of your body like a car. Without fuel, a car won't run properly. Your body is the same way. Without breakfast, your body doesn't run the way that it should.

3   Experts agree that kids who eat breakfast do better on tests and pay more attention in class than kids who skip the first meal of the day. Studies also show that kids who eat breakfast have more energy for after-school sports and clubs.

4   A healthy breakfast should include of some sort of protein (such as meats, eggs, or beans), whole grains (usually from breads or oatmeal), fruits or vegetables, and a dairy product (milk, cheese, or yogurt). A balanced breakfast helps you start the day right. Too much sugar can leave you feeling tired and hungry in a few hours, so be sure to avoid cereals with large amounts of sugar.

5   So, before you head out the door, take a break for breakfast. You can even help prepare your own meals. This delicious omelet recipe is a quick and easy way to get the fuel you need for a fabulous day!

Veggie Lover's Omelet

6   Who says you can't eat vegetables in the morning? This tasty recipe helps you get a serving of the vegetables you need every day to stay healthy. Before you start, ask an adult for help. You will need to use a stove, which can be dangerous. Let the adult handle the stove—and get ready to get cooking!

Ingredients:

3 egg whites

You can buy a package of egg whites at the grocery store, or you can ask your adult helper to aid you in separating the egg whites from the yolks.

1 oz. low-fat shredded cheese

You can use whatever cheese you like best. Cheddar and Swiss cheese taste great in this omelet!

½ cup veggies

Pick the veggies that you love. Chopped broccoli and spinach are good choices. Mushrooms are yummy as well! You can even spice things up with some red or green peppers and diced tomatoes.

¼ cup of low-fat milk

Cooking spray

Utensils:

A medium pan

A spatula

A large bowl

A whisk

Step 1: Spray a medium pan with the cooking spray. Ask your adult helper to heat the pan over a low flame on the stove.

Step 2: While the adult is heating the pan, you can mix the milk and egg whites together in the bowl, using a whisk.

Step 3: Once you have mixed the eggs and milk, have the adult help pour the mixture in the pan.

Step 4: While the eggs are cooking, measure your vegetables.

Step 5: Have the adult help you add the vegetables to the omelet.

Step 6: Just before the omelet is finished cooking, sprinkle cheese over the omelet.

Step 7: Ask the adult to flip one side of the omelet over, using the spatula.

Step 8: Once the eggs are cooked all the way through, you're ready to eat! Remember to remind the adult helper to turn off the stove and ask him or her to put the omelet on a plate for you.

Your breakfast is ready to eat! You might want to add a piece of whole wheat toast and a few slices of fruit to make your meal complete. These foods will help you to make the most out of your day!

⁇ Questions ⁇

1. **Why did the author write this passage?**

   Ⓐ to tell a story about a kid eating breakfast

   Ⓑ to explain why some cereals are bad for you

   Ⓒ to encourage readers to eat a healthy breakfast

   Ⓓ to describe to readers what an omelet looks like

 HINT

This question asks you to think about the entire passage. What do you think the author wanted the reader to know? Think about this and then choose the best answer.

2. **With which sentence would the author most likely agree?**

   Ⓐ It is okay to sleep through breakfast on the weekends.

   Ⓑ Sugary foods like doughnuts should be avoided at breakfast.

   Ⓒ It is okay to skip breakfast if you are running late for school.

   Ⓓ Sugary cereal is perfect to eat before you go to school.

 HINT

Think about how the author feels about eating breakfast and the types of foods that you should eat at breakfast. Pick the sentence that doesn't fit what the author says in the passage.

3. In paragraph 6, what does the author mean when she says "Who says you can't eat vegetables in the morning"?

Ⓐ Someone told the author vegetables don't taste good in omelets.

Ⓑ Someone told the author not to eat vegetables in the morning.

Ⓒ Most people don't like eating any kind of vegetable.

Ⓓ Many people don't eat many vegetables in the morning.

 HINT

Reread paragraph 6 if you need some help. Look for clues about what the author means in the paragraph and then choose the best answer.

4. What is the purpose of the recipe in this passage?

Ⓐ to convince you to eat more vegetables

Ⓑ to make you want to eat breakfast

Ⓒ to teach you how to make an omelet

Ⓓ to describe what an omelet tastes like

 HINT

Look back at the recipe. Why is it there and what do you learn from it?

Passage 2

Read this passage and answer the questions that follow. Use the hint below each question to help you choose the correct answer.

New Jersey's Pine Barrens

Long ago, much of New Jersey was a giant forest. The Native Americans who first lived there could not even build homes in the forest—there were too many trees in the way! The thickest forest of all was in an area called the Pine Barrens. The Pine Barrens have changed a lot over the years, but you can still see this amazing place today.

The Pine Barrens is a huge piece of land that stretches across southern New Jersey. Large roads pass through the Pine Barrens. These roads connect New York, Philadelphia, and the beaches of New Jersey. Millions of people travel through the Pine Barrens each year, but not many of them know the story of the ancient land.

The great forests of the Pine Barrens grew because of the soil. The soil in the area is called "sugar sand," because it looks like grains of sugar, or sand from the beach. Not many plants could grow in the grainy ground—but trees could. For a very long time, great trees grew high into the sky.

The first people to see these trees, the Native Americans, were amazed. The Native Americans loved the forest even though they could not live inside it. The forest was filled with animals, from deer to bear to beaver, which the people could hunt for food. The forest was also a beautiful place to visit. There weren't only pine trees. There were also hickory, oak, chestnut, and ash trees. The many kinds of trees, and the colorful flowers that grew beneath them, were lovely to see.

When settlers moved into the area, they were just as surprised, but they soon grew disappointed. Most of the settlers were farmers, and they wanted to grow crops like corn and beans on the land. The grainy, sandy soil would not let these crops grow. The settlers looked for other ways to use the land. They soon realized that the trees themselves would be very useful.

Settlers began cutting down some trees to use for building many different things. They even learned to use old trees that had already fallen down. This was called "shingle mining." Workers would dig into the ground to find giant trees that had fallen hundreds of years before. The workers would "mine" the buried trees, taking out great amounts of timber. The wood from these ancient trees was used in making boards, barrels, and boats. Most famously, this wood was used to make wooden shingles for the roofs of houses.

Many businesses began in and around the Pine Barrens. Settlers built sawmills, buildings in which trees are cut into planks of wood. People also made paper mills, where some of the wood could be turned into paper for writing and reading. Still other people used the wood to make factories for glass and charcoal.

The Pine Barrens held other surprises for the settlers. In some areas between the trees were great swamps called bogs. People looking in the water of these bogs found ore, or lumps of metal. This metal was known as "bog iron." People mined bog iron from the swamps for many years. The bog iron was melted down and turned into all sorts of things. Much of the iron was used to make tools and weapons for soldiers during the Revolutionary War.

Many of the mines and factories in the Pine Barrens are empty today. People gave up working in them, and plants and trees grew back to cover the buildings. Some businesses are still operating there, though. One old business, the Batsto Iron Works, is still standing today. In fact, people have saved this historic factory and the many homes around it.

The Batsto Iron Works began in 1766, when Charles Read set up some mills in the Pine Barrens. Read mined for bog iron, and he also turned wood into charcoal. Then he used the charcoal to melt down the bog iron! Read and his partners made cooking pots and kettles and soldiers' weapons that were used in America's war for independence.

Workers and their families moved to the Pine Barrens and made a village near the Iron Works. Although the Iron Works went out of business, people kept living in the village for many years. Instead of letting Batsto Village fade away, people decided to save it. They made a park out of the land, and visitors can go there to see the original factories and village.

Today laws are in place to protect the trees of the Pine Barrens. People want the trees to grow tall and beautiful again for future people to enjoy. At the same time, the Pine Barrens is still a very useful place. People have found that cranberries grow in the bogs. The soil in the area is also great for blueberry farms. Today the Pine Barrens area produces much of the country's cranberries and blueberries.

The next time you or your friends travel through the forests of southern New Jersey, you can think about the long history of the Pine Barrens.

⁇ Questions ⁇

1. **Why does the author most likely include the description in paragraph 2?**

    Ⓐ to explain the story of an ancient place

    Ⓑ to tell why trees grow so well in the Pine Barrens

    Ⓒ to show where you can find the Pine Barrens

    Ⓓ to compare different cities near New Jersey

 HINT

This question asks you about just one paragraph from the passage. Look back and find the second paragraph. What does it tell you? What reason would the author have to give you that information?

2. **Why did the author write this passage?**

    Ⓐ to explain the history of the Pine Barrens

    Ⓑ to contrast the Pine Barrens with other forests

    Ⓒ to persuade people to visit the Pine Barrens

    Ⓓ to describe the many plants of the Pine Barrens

HINT

> Think about the entire passage in order to answer this question. What was the main idea in the passage? What was the author trying to do when he wrote this passage?

3. **With which sentence would the author most likely agree?**

    Ⓐ Factories are more important than forests.

    Ⓑ Forests can be useful and beautiful.

    Ⓒ More logging is needed in the Pine Barrens.

    Ⓓ Beaches are more interesting than forests.

HINT

> Read each of these statements. Think about what you've learned about the author of the passage. Which statement would he most likely believe is correct?

Passage 3

Read this passage and answer the questions that follow. Use the hint below each question to help you choose the correct answer.

Excerpt from *Rebecca of Sunnybrook Farm*

by Kate Douglas Wiggin

The old stage coach was rumbling along the dusty road that runs from Maplewood to Riverboro. The day was as warm as midsummer, though it was only the middle of May, and Mr. Jeremiah Cobb was favoring the horses as much as possible, yet never losing sight of the fact that he carried the mail. The hills were many, and the reins lay loosely in his hands as he lolled back in his seat and extended one foot and leg luxuriously over the dashboard. His brimmed hat of worn felt was well pulled over his eyes, and he revolved a quid of tobacco in his left cheek.

There was one passenger in the coach,—a small dark-haired person in a glossy buff calico dress. She was so slender and so stiffly starched that she slid from space to space on the leather cushions, though she braced herself against the middle seat with her feet and extended her cotton-gloved hands on each side, in order to maintain some sort of balance. Whenever the wheels sank farther than usual into a rut, or jolted suddenly over a stone, she bounded involuntarily into the air, came down again, pushed back her funny little straw hat, and picked up or settled more firmly a small pink sun shade, which seemed to be her chief responsibility, —unless we except a bead purse, into which she looked whenever the condition of the roads would permit, finding great apparent satisfaction in that its precious contents neither disappeared nor grew less. Mr. Cobb guessed nothing of these harassing details of travel, his business being to carry people to their destinations, not, necessarily, to make them comfortable on the way. Indeed he had forgotten the very existence of this one unnoteworthy little passenger.

When he was about to leave the post-office in Maplewood that morning, a woman had alighted from a wagon, and coming up to him, inquired whether this were the Riverboro stage, and if he were Mr. Cobb. Being answered in the affirmative, she nodded to a child who was eagerly waiting for the answer, and who ran towards her as if she feared to be a moment too late. The child might have been ten or eleven years old perhaps, but whatever the number of her summers, she had an air of being small for her age. Her mother helped her into the stage coach, deposited a bundle and a bouquet of lilacs beside her, superintended the "roping on" behind of an old hair trunk, and finally paid the fare, counting out the silver with great care.

"I want you should take her to my sisters' in Riverboro," she said. "Do you know Mirandy and Jane Sawyer? They live in the brick house."

Lord bless your soul, he knew 'em as well as if he'd made 'em!

"Well, she's going there, and they're expecting her. Will you keep an eye on her, please? If she can get out anywhere and get with folks, or get anybody in to keep her company, she'll do it. Good-by, Rebecca; try not to get into any mischief, and sit quiet, so you'll look neat an' nice when you get there. Don't be any trouble to Mr. Cobb.—You see, she's kind of excited.— We came on the cars from Temperance yesterday, slept all night at my cousin's, and drove from her house—eight miles it is—this morning."

"Good-by, mother, don't worry; you know it isn't as if I hadn't traveled before."

The woman gave a short sardonic laugh and said in an explanatory way to Mr. Cobb, "She's been to Wareham and stayed over night; that isn't much to be journey-proud on!"

"IT WAS TRAVELING, mother," said the child eagerly and willfully. "It was leaving the farm, and putting up lunch in a basket, and a little riding and a little steam cars, and we carried our nightgowns."

"Don't tell the whole village about it, if we did," said the mother, interrupting the reminiscences of this experienced voyager. "Haven't I told you before," she whispered, in a last attempt at discipline, "that you shouldn't talk about night-gowns and stockings and—things like that, in a loud tone of voice, and especially when there's men folks round?"

"I know, mother, I know, and I won't. All I want to say is"—here Mr. Cobb gave a cluck, slapped the reins, and the horses started sedately on their daily task—"all I want to say is that it is a journey when"—the stage was really under way now and Rebecca had to put her head out of the window over the door in order to finish her sentence—"it IS a journey when you carry a nightgown!"

The objectionable word, uttered in a high treble, floated back to the offended ears of Mrs. Randall, who watched the stage out of sight, gathered up her packages from the bench at the store door, and stepped into the wagon that had been standing at the hitching-post. As she turned the horse's head toward home she rose to her feet for a moment, and shading her eyes with her hand, looked at a cloud of dust in the dim distance.

"Mirandy'll have her hands full, I guess," she said to herself; "but I shouldn't wonder if it would be the making of Rebecca."

Questions

1. **Why did the author most likely write this passage?**

    Ⓐ to teach readers a lesson about having good manners

    Ⓑ to tell readers a story about a little girl going on a trip

    Ⓒ to describe what it was like to ride in a wagon

    Ⓓ to inform readers about the way children used to travel

 HINT

Is this fiction or nonfiction? Why do you think the author wrote this passage?

2. **The purpose of the second paragraph of this passage is to**

Ⓐ tell readers how Mr. Cobb treats his passengers.

Ⓑ help readers predict what will happen next.

Ⓒ describe what it is like to ride in a coach.

Ⓓ explain where the coach was going.

HINT

Reread this paragraph. It is about a young woman. But why did the author include it?

3. **What do you think will happen next? Use details from the story to support your answer.**

_____

_____

_____

_____

_____

Chapter 5

Conclusions and Opinions

Clusters

A1 Questioning, Clarifying, Predicting   These questions draw on students' use of reading strategies to construct meaning. The questions introduce a focus and a context for responding (asking a question of the author or a character, for example) and ask students to select and analyze ideas and information from the text to develop a response. Given the nature of this task, these questions are almost always open-ended.

A3 Forming Opinions about Text and Author's Techniques   These questions elicit students' response to aspects of the text. The questions introduce a focus (such as whether the main character would make a good friend) and ask students to select and analyze ideas and information from the text to develop a response. Given the nature of this task, opinion questions are always open-ended. At times, students are asked to identify techniques the author uses to convey a particular point of view or bias.

A4 Making Judgments, Drawing Conclusions   These questions ask students to draw conclusions based on knowledge they have garnered from the ideas and information within the text. Students might be asked to analyze how the setting (the season of the year, for example) affects the sequence of events within a story, or to analyze the effect of skipping a step in a certain procedure.

Introduction

For some questions on the New Jersey ASK, you will have to draw a **conclusion**, which is a judgment about something. It's what you think based on what you have read. You won't find the answer to this kind of question in the passage. You will have to think about what you have read and then choose the right answer.

When you answer questions asking you to draw conclusions, it might help to imagine that you are a detective in search of clues. Look for clues in the passage to help you answer the question.

In real life, you probably draw conclusions without even realizing it. Imagine that you see your friend crying. You would conclude that your friend is sad. Imagine that one of your new shoes is chewed to bits. You might conclude that your dog, Flea, chewed your shoe.

For other questions on this test, you will have to form an **opinion**, which is what you think about something. Your opinion should be based on what you have read and should make sense based on the details in the passage.

Practice Passage

Read this passage and answer the questions that follow:

Going to the Playground

Although she normally picked at her peas, today Jillian hurried to finish her dinner. Her parents suggested that she slow down and let her food digest. Jillian usually didn't want to eat her vegetables, but today she quickly shoveled everything into her mouth. She was too excited to fuss over the taste. Billy had promised to take her and her best friend, Annie, to the large playground on the other side of town.

This playground was Jillian's favorite. There was so much to do there! She could kick her legs back and forth to fly high on the swing set, ride the merry-go-round, or play a game of hopscotch.

As soon as she finished eating, Jillian scrambled to the front door, where Billy and Annie were already waiting in the driveway with their bikes.

"Are you ready to go?" Annie asked cheerfully.

Jillian's mom gave her a bike helmet. "Be careful to stay near Billy," she reminded Jillian, "and listen to whatever he tells you to do."

1. **Who is Billy?**

   Ⓐ Jillian's brother

   Ⓑ someone older

   Ⓒ Annie's father

   Ⓓ Jillian's best friend

Think about what you know about Billy from the story. He is taking Annie and Jillian to a park on the other side of town. And Jillian's mother tells Jillian to stay by him and do whatever he says to do. He is probably not Jillian's brother (answer choice A), because he is waiting outside with Annie. He is definitely someone older, so answer choice B is probably the right answer. He is probably

not Annie's father (answer choice C), because he is riding a bike with Annie, and Jillian calls him "Billy." Annie is Jillian's best friend, so answer choice D is best.

2. **After reading the story, what can you tell about Jillian's parents?**

   Ⓐ They are happy when she eats quickly.

   Ⓑ They want Jillian to go to the park near home.

   Ⓒ They don't like her to go bike riding.

   Ⓓ They want Jillian to be safe.

Think about what you know about Jillian's parents from the story. You know that they want her to take her time eating her food. So answer choice A is not correct. They are letting her go to the park across town, so answer choice B is also incorrect. Answer choice C is also incorrect. They are letting her go bike riding. Answer choice D is the best answer. Her mother gives her a bike helmet which is for her safety and also tells her to listen to Billy.

3. **Do you think Jillian will have fun in the playground? Why or why not? Use information from the story to support your response. Write your answer in the space below.**

_____

_____

_____

_____

Think about how the story begins. Jillian sounds like she normally enjoys the playground. The story also tells about how Jillian likes being with Billy and Annie.

Passage 1

Read this passage and answer the questions that follow. Use the hint below each question to help you choose the correct answer.

A Giant Discovery

In the mid-1800s, a scientist named William Parker Foulke was on vacation in Haddonfield, New Jersey, when he learned that a few years earlier someone had found an enormous bone buried under a local farm. Foulke believed that the giant bone might belong to a dinosaur. At the time, people didn't know much about dinosaurs. Some people did not even believe that dinosaurs were real.

Foulke examined the huge bone and instantly became interested. Foulke hired diggers, and they spent the rest of the summer and much of the fall excavating the mysterious giant bones. When they were done, they had found the entire skeleton of an animal that seemed to be a combination of a lizard and a bird. This was the first whole dinosaur skeleton found in the world! The animal was named *Hadrosaurus foulkii*, which comes from the name of the town where the bones were found and the name of the man who made the discovery.

The bones were taken to the Philadelphia Academy of Natural Sciences, where they were put together. The assembled dinosaur was shown to the public as proof that dinosaurs were real at one time. Until this point people knew very little about dinosaurs. In Europe, some people had found dinosaur fossils here and there, but this was the first discovery of an entire skeleton, and people's understanding of the past suddenly changed.

News of the massive animal spread quickly. All over the world, curiosity grew. People wanted to learn all about dinosaurs. Before this time, people suspected that giant creatures had once lived on earth, but before Foulke's discovery, they had no idea of what the creatures looked like or how large they truly were. For many years the Philadelphia Academy of Natural Sciences was the only place on the planet to see an assembled skeleton of a dinosaur.

From Foulke's discovery, scientists learned many facts about dinosaurs. They found that some dinosaurs walked on two legs. Until this point, scientists had thought dinosaurs walked on four legs like lizards. Most of what scientists knew about dinosaurs was only guessed until Foulke's discovery in Haddonfield.

In 1971, Haddonfield's mayor gave the key to the city to the *Hadrosaurus foulkii*. The mayor also named the dinosaur an honorary citizen. Today a small stone marks the site of the discovery. In 1991, the *Hadrosaurus foulkii* became the official state dinosaur of New Jersey. The *Hadrosaurus foulkii* skeleton that Foulke and his men excavated is still on display at the Philadelphia Academy of Natural Sciences.

Questions

1. **Why did people mark the site of the dinosaur discovery with a small stone?**

   Ⓐ to show where the bones were found

   Ⓑ to show that other dinosaurs might be there

   Ⓒ to make people want to see the dinosaur

   Ⓓ to tell people where to go to see the dinosaur

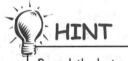
HINT
Reread the last paragraph of this passage.

2. **How did the mayor of Haddonfield feel about the dinosaur skeleton?**

   Ⓐ concerned

   Ⓑ upset

   Ⓒ bored

   Ⓓ excited

HINT
Remember that the mayor gave the key to the city to the dinosaur.

3. What made this dinosaur skeleton more important than others discovered before it? Use details from the passage to support your answer.

_____

_____

_____

_____

_____

_____

_____

_____

_____

_____

_____

_____

_____

HINT

Reread the passage to look for clues about what may have made this skeleton an especially important discovery.

Passage 2

Read this passage and answer the questions that follow. Use the hint below each question to help you choose the correct answer.

The Cape May Lighthouse

Have you ever seen the Cape May Lighthouse? This extremely tall structure stands nearly 160 feet high. To get to the top of the lighthouse, you have to climb 199 stairs! The Cape May Lighthouse stands proudly at the southern tip of New Jersey.

The lighthouse was built over a hundred years ago to help ships sail safely along the coast and into the Delaware Bay. When the lighthouse was built, there wasn't yet electricity, so a person called the lighthouse keeper used to live near the lighthouse. The keeper climbed the stairs each evening to light oil lamps behind special lenses, which made the light look a special way when it flashed. It was the keeper's job to make sure the oil lamps stayed lit. This was an important job, because ships passing by needed the light from the lighthouse to navigate their way in the water in the dark.

The Cape May Lighthouse that is there today wasn't the first. The very first lighthouse used to stand in a nearby place that is now underwater. This lighthouse was built back around 1785, but the shore underneath the lighthouse washed away over time. Old writings say that the bottom of the lighthouse was underwater each day during high tide. Some people claim that after a storm, pieces of brick from this lighthouse sometimes wash up on the shore. Wouldn't it be great to find one of these?

When this lighthouse was taken down, a second lighthouse was built on the bluff in a higher place, but this lighthouse didn't last very long either. As with the first lighthouse, the ground underneath it began to wash away, and the lighthouse itself also began to fall apart. Old writings say that the keeper of this lighthouse wasn't experienced and didn't know how to take care of a lighthouse. The weather near the ocean can get very rough, and a lighthouse can be easily damaged. Repairs have to be made right away to keep it in good condition.

This second lighthouse was taken down, and a third was built about 600 feet away. This is the lighthouse that stands today. The way a lighthouse flashes its lights is called its characteristic. And the way a lighthouse is painted is called its daymark. Each lighthouse has a different characteristic and daymark. This lets ship captains know exactly where they are. The Cape May Lighthouse's characteristic is that it flashes a light every fifteen seconds. This light can be seen twenty-four miles out to sea. The tower of the lighthouse, the tall part, is bright white. The lantern, the top part, is bright red. This color combination is the Cape May Lighthouse's daymark.

Today the Cape May Lighthouse no longer has oil lamps and is lit with electricity. A keeper doesn't take care of it anymore. The U.S. Coast Guard makes sure that the lighthouse stays in good condition and its lights shine brightly out to sea each night to help keep ships safe. People visit the Cape May Lighthouse nearly every day from April through November. If they are up to the challenge, they can climb the many stairs and enjoy a beautiful view of the Cape May peninsula.

Questions

1. **Why was the third lighthouse built in a different place?**

    Ⓐ so it could be seen more easily by ship captains

    Ⓑ because it had a different daymark and characteristic

    Ⓒ so it would be safe from the ground washing away

    Ⓓ because the first two lighthouses were still there

HINT

Remember what happened to the first two lighthouses.

2. **Why doesn't a keeper take care of the lighthouse now?**

   Ⓐ There isn't as much for a keeper to do.

   Ⓑ Keepers are hard to find today.

   Ⓒ The last keeper didn't do a good job.

   Ⓓ The lighthouse stays in good condition.

**HINT**

Reread the last paragraph for a clue.

3. **What is probably the reason the lighthouse isn't open in the winter?**

   Ⓐ The lighthouse is repaired during this time.

   Ⓑ The lighthouse is not used during this time.

   Ⓒ It is very cold by the lighthouse during this time.

   Ⓓ The stairs are harder to climb during this time.

**HINT**

Do you think a lot of people are on the beach during the winter?

4. **Do you think it would be fun to visit the Cape May Lighthouse? Why or why not?**

   _____

   _____

   _____

   _____

   _____

Passage 3

Read the passage and answer the following questions. Use the hint underneath each question to help you choose the correct answer.

Maria Tallchief

Maria Tallchief was a very famous ballerina. Maria was born in 1925 on a Native American reservation in Oklahoma. Her father was the chief of the Osage tribe. Her mother was Scottish and Irish. Maria spent the first eight years of her life in Oklahoma. She loved spending time outdoors. Her favorite pastime was playing in the pasture near the horses. Maria also loved to sing and dance. She enjoyed pretending that she was a great star. Her mother encouraged Maria to learn all she could about music. Maria and her sister, Marjorie, began taking piano lessons when Maria was only four.

Later, Maria took dance lessons. She was very good at dancing. Her family thought she might really become a star one day. When she was twelve, she and her family left Oklahoma. They moved to California, where there were better dance teachers.

Maria had a new dance teacher in California who had once been a famous ballerina in Russia. She believed that Maria could be a great ballerina, too, but she wasn't happy with what Maria had learned at her old dance school. She was shocked that Maria was already wearing pointe shoes, which have metal in the tip. Ballerinas wear these shoes to make it look as if they are standing on their toes. Maria's teacher said Maria was not yet ready to wear pointe shoes. She told Maria to forget everything that she had been taught so she could relearn everything the right way. Maria felt sad when she heard this, but she was determined to learn.

This teacher made Maria work very hard and spend many hours practicing. She had little time to do anything else. Her teacher once told her, "When you sleep, you sleep like a ballerina." She even said that Maria should stand like a ballerina when she was on the street waiting for the bus!

Maria studied with this teacher for five years and then moved to New York City. A new ballet company there was looking for ballerinas to dance with them. Maria auditioned for this group, which means that she danced for them. When they saw Maria dance, they were amazed. Maria was one of the best dancers they had ever seen, and they asked her to be part of their group.

Soon Maria was dancing on stage in front of many people, often in the lead role. She became very famous. Before long, Maria traveled to other countries to dance for the people there. Millions of people around the world wanted to see Maria dance. Maria became a prima ballerina, which means that she was the lead dancer in a ballet company.

Maria was a prima ballerina for eighteen years before she decided to devote her life to teaching young people how to dance. She and her sister Marjorie started their own ballet company called the Chicago City Ballet. "A ballerina takes steps given to her and makes them her own," Maria once said. She taught her students how to perform dance steps correctly, but she also encouraged them to make the steps their own. Maria wrote an autobiography about her life as a dancer called *Maria Tallchief: America's Prima Ballerina*.

Questions

1. **What can you tell about Maria's dance teachers in Oklahoma?**

   Ⓐ They were sure that Maria would be a star.

   Ⓑ They did not want Maria to wear pointe shoes.

   Ⓒ They did not know as much as they should.

   Ⓓ They had once been prima ballerinas.

HINT

Reread what happened to Maria when she moved to California.

2. **Do you think Maria would make a good dance teacher? Why or why not?**

   Write your answer on the lines below.

   _____

   _____

   _____

   _____

   _____

HINT

Reread the last paragraph of the article and then form your own opinion.

3. Maria's family helps her become a dancer.

   • Explain how her family helped her.

   • Decide what they did that was most helpful, and explain why.

   Use information from the story to support your response.

   Write your answer on the lines below.

   _____

   _____

   _____

   _____

   _____

   _____

   _____

   _____

   _____

   _____

   _____

   _____

HINT

Reread the article and look for the ways that Maria's family helped her become a dancer. Then use your own judgment to choose the most important way.

Chapter 6

Literature (Made-Up Stories)

Clusters

A5   Interpreting Textual Conventions and Literary Elements   These questions focus on devices used by the author. Students might be asked to analyze what a specific metaphor conveys about a character in the story, for example, or why an author uses italics for certain words.

W5   Recognizing Text Organization   Text organization encompasses the patterns of organization that characterize the respective genres. For the narratives, questions focusing on setting, character, and plot as well as on any distinctive pattern within the story, such as repetition.

Introduction

On the NJ ASK, you will be asked questions about made-up stories. These stories have characters, a setting, and a plot.

Before authors begin writing, they put a lot of thought into the stories they write. They plan out how the characters will act, where they are from, and what will happen in the story a long time before they put anything down on paper. When authors want to make something stand out, they will do something special with the text, like put it in *italics*. This is the author's way of letting the reader know that this part of the story is important. This chapter will help you learn more about made-up stories.

Setting

The **setting** is where the action of the story or poem takes place. The setting of a story could be a school, someone's house, or even another planet. Read this paragraph:

Mandy passed by many cages filled with wagging tails. All of the dogs were so cute and playful that she wasn't sure which one to choose. She wanted to take all of them home with her, but she could pick only one. Suddenly, Mandy saw a black and white dog with a happy face. He almost looked as if he were smiling at Mandy. She walked over to the cage and let him lick her hand. Mandy knew she had found her dog.

Where does this story take place? There are many clues in the paragraph to help you. If you're thinking that Mandy is at an animal shelter, you're correct!

Characters

Made-up stories have characters in them. **Characters** can be people, animals, or even things. Because these stories are made-up, the author can make bears or chairs talk and walk, if he or she wants to. Characters say and do things in the story. The **main character** is the character that does and says the most in a story. Stories may have more than one main character.

Read this short story:

A Helping Hand

As Paul started walking home from school, it began to rain. Paul was happy that he had listened to his father that morning and grabbed an umbrella before leaving the house. The wind was blowing and the rain was coming down so hard that it was hard for Paul to see. *At least I'm dry,* thought Paul. Finally, the rain let up a little bit.

As he hurried to make it home before the rain became heavy again, he saw someone walking ahead of him. It was one of the boys from his class. The boy's name was David. It was obvious that David had not remembered an umbrella, because he was holding his jacket over his head to stay dry.

Paul walked over to David and asked him if he wanted to share his umbrella. Paul walked with David to his house. When the boys arrived, David thanked Paul for his help and asked him if he wanted to come over and play video games sometime. Paul thought that that sounded like a fun idea.

Write the names of the two characters in this story on the lines below.

_____

_____

Plot

What happens in the story is known as the **plot**. The main events of a story make up the story's plot. These events move from the beginning of the story to the end. In many made-up stories, the main character has some sort of problem. This problem is a part of the plot. What the character does about this problem is also part of the plot.

In the story "A Helping Hand," David's problem is that he does not have an umbrella and it has started to rain. His problem is solved when Paul offers to share his umbrella with David. These are the major events in the story:

1. On the way home from school, it begins to rain.

2. Paul takes out his umbrella.

3. Paul sees David, who has forgotten to bring an umbrella.

4. Paul walks David to his house.

5. David asks Paul if he wants to play video games sometime.

Special Language and Type

Authors will sometimes use special language in their stories or poems. They might also use special type such as all CAPITAL LETTERS, *italics*, or **boldface** lettering. Read this story:

Whenever Beth felt upset or angry, she would go into her room and write down her feelings in a worn-looking journal. The journal always helped her to sort everything out in her mind. Beth picked up the brown book. "Hello, dear old friend. I have a story for you!" Beth grabbed a pen and began writing. *I cannot believe what my brother did today! Sometimes he makes me so angry. . . .*

1. **Why do you think the author put certain words in italics?**

   _____

2. **Why does Beth call her journal her "dear old friend"?**

   _____

Passage 1

Read the story below. Then answer the questions about the story. Use the hints underneath each question to help you choose the right answer.

Excerpt from *O Pioneers!*

by Willa Cather

One Sunday afternoon in July . . . Carl . . . heard the rattle of a wagon along the hill road. Looking up he recognized the Bergsons' team, with two seats in the wagon, which meant they were off for a pleasure excursion. Oscar and Lou, on the front seat, wore their cloth hats and coats, never worn except on Sundays, and Emil, on the second seat with Alexandra, sat proudly in his new trousers, made from a pair of his father's, and a pink-striped shirt, with a wide ruffled collar. Oscar stopped the horses and waved to Carl, who caught up his hat and ran through the melon patch to join them.

"Want to go with us?" Lou called. "We're going to Crazy Ivar's to buy a hammock."

"Sure." Carl ran up panting, and clambering over the wheel sat down beside Emil. "I've always wanted to see Ivar's pond. They say it's the biggest in all the country . . ."

Emil grinned. "I'd be awful scared to go," he admitted, "if you big boys weren't along to take care of me. Did you ever hear him howl, Carl? People say sometimes he runs about the country howling at night . . .

". . . I'd be too scared to run," Emil admitted mournfully, twisting his fingers. "I guess I'd sit right down on the ground . . ."

The big boys laughed . . .

"He wouldn't hurt you, Emil," said Carl persuasively. "He came to doctor our mare when she ate green corn and swelled up most as big as the water-tank. He petted her just like you do your cats. I couldn't understand much he said, for he don't talk any English, but he kept patting her and groaning as if he had the pain himself, and saying, 'There now, sister, that's easier, that's better!'"

Lou and Oscar laughed, and Emil giggled delightedly and looked up at his sister.

"I don't think he knows anything at all about doctoring," said Oscar scornfully. "They say when horses have distemper he takes the medicine himself . . . "

Alexandra spoke up. "That's what the Crows said, but he cured their horses, all the same. Some days his mind is cloudy, like. But if you can get him on a clear day, you can learn a great deal from him. He understands animals. Didn't I see him take the horn off the Berquists' cow when she had torn it loose and went crazy? . . . Ivar came running with his white bag, and the moment he got to her she was quiet . . . "

Emil had been watching his sister, his face reflecting the sufferings of the cow. "And then didn't it hurt her any more?" he asked.

Alexandra patted him. "No, not any more. And in two days they could use her milk again."

The road to Ivar's homestead was a very poor one. He had settled in the rough country across the county line. . . . Ivar had explained his choice by saying that the fewer neighbors he had, the fewer temptations.

Nevertheless, when one considered that his chief business was horse-doctoring, it seemed rather short-sighted of him to live in the most inaccessible place he could find . . .

Lou sniffed. "Whoever heard of him talking sense, anyhow! I'd rather have ducks for supper than Crazy Ivar's tongue."

Emil was alarmed. "Oh, but, Lou, you don't want to make him mad! He might howl!"

They all laughed again. . . . They had left the lagoons and the red grass behind them. In Crazy Ivar's country the grass was short and gray . . . The wild flowers disappeared, and only in the bottom of the draws and gullies grew a few of the very toughest and hardiest: shoestring, and ironweed, and snow-on-the-mountain.

Questions

1. **Who is the story's main character?**

   (A) Emil

   (B) Carl

   (C) Crazy Ivar

   (D) Lou

   HINT

   Think about the person that does and says the most in the story. This is the main character.

2. **When does most of this story take place?**

   (A) in the winter

   (B) in the spring

   (C) in the summer

   (D) in the fall

   HINT

   Reread the first few lines of the story. These lines tell you during which season the story takes place.

3. **Where does most of this story take place?**

   (A) in a field

   (B) on a wagon

   (C) on a farm

   (D) in a classroom

   HINT

   Think about what the characters in the story are doing. This will help you to figure out where most of this passage takes place.

Passage 2

Read the story below. Then answer the questions about the story. Use the hints underneath each question to help you choose the right answer.

Excerpt from *The Selfish Giant*

by Oscar Wilde

Every afternoon, as they were coming from school, the children used to go and play in the Giant's garden.

It was a large lovely garden, with soft green grass. Here and there over the grass stood beautiful flowers like stars, and there were twelve peach-trees that in the spring-time broke out into delicate blossoms of pink and pearl, and in the autumn bore rich fruit. The birds sat on the trees and sang so sweetly that the children used to stop their games in order to listen to them. "How happy we are here!" they cried to each other.

One day the Giant came back. He had been to visit his friend the Cornish ogre, and had stayed with him for seven years. After the seven years were over he had said all that he had to say, for his conversation was limited, and he determined to return to his own castle. When he arrived he saw the children playing in the garden.

"What are you doing here?" he cried in a very gruff voice, and the children ran away.

"My own garden is my own garden," said the Giant; "any one can understand that, and I will allow nobody to play in it but myself." So he built a high wall all round it, and put up a notice-board.

Trespassers will be Prosecuted

He was a very selfish Giant.

The poor children had now nowhere to play. They tried to play on the road, but the road was very dusty and full of hard stones, and they did not like it. They used to wander round the high wall when their lessons were over, and talk about the beautiful garden inside. "How happy we were there," they said to each other.

Then the Spring came, and all over the country there were little blossoms and little birds. Only in the garden of the Selfish Giant it was still winter. The birds did not care to sing in it as there were no children, and the trees forgot to blossom. Once a beautiful flower put its head out from the grass, but when it saw the notice-board it was so sorry for the children that it slipped back into the ground again, and went off to sleep. The only people who were pleased were the Snow and the Frost. "Spring has forgotten this garden," they cried, "so we will live here all the year round." The Snow covered up the grass with her great white cloak, and the Frost painted all the trees silver. Then they invited the North Wind to stay with them, and he came. He was wrapped in furs, and he roared all day about the garden, and blew the chimney-pots down. "This is a delightful spot," he said, "we must ask the Hail on a visit." So the Hail came. Every day for three hours he rattled on the roof of the castle till he broke most of the slates, and then he ran round and round the garden as fast as he could go. He was dressed in grey, and his breath was like ice.

"I cannot understand why the Spring is so late in coming," said the Selfish Giant, as he sat at the window and looked out at his cold white garden; "I hope there will be a change in the weather."

But the Spring never came, nor the Summer. The Autumn gave golden fruit to every garden, but to the Giant's garden she gave none. "He is too selfish," she said. So it was always Winter there, and the North Wind, and the Hail, and the Frost, and the Snow danced about through the trees.

Questions

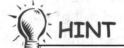

1. **Who is the story's main character?**

   Ⓐ Frost

   Ⓑ Snow

   Ⓒ the North Wind

   Ⓓ the Selfish Giant

HINT

Look at all of the answer choices. Which character is this story mostly about?

2. **Some words in the story are written in capital letters to show that**

   Ⓐ the Giant is angry with the children.

   Ⓑ the Giant is speaking to the children.

   Ⓒ the sign warns people to stay away.

   Ⓓ the sign tells people to come back later.

HINT

Think about where the words are and what they mean. This will help you to understand why the words are written in capital letters.

3. **Which part of this story tells you that this story is make-believe?**

   Ⓐ The children play in the garden.

   Ⓑ The children go to school.

   Ⓒ The seasons begin to change.

   Ⓓ Snow and Frost can talk.

HINT

This question asks you to think about the part of the story that could not really happen. This is the part that lets you know that the story is make-believe.

Passage 3

Read the story below. Then answer the questions about the story. Use the hints underneath each question to help you choose the right answer.

Making a Big Sound

Jason waited excitedly at his desk. Today was the day that his music teacher, Ms. Chase, would give everyone an instrument to play in the school's music show. The students would take their instruments home to learn their parts, and then practice together during music class.

I hope that I get an interesting instrument to play, like a guitar! thought Jason as he waited patiently. Perhaps he would play the trumpet or the saxophone. He also thought that it might be fun to bang on the drums. There was also a flute, a trombone, and many other instruments for the students to play. Jason dreamed of standing out during the music show.

Ms. Chase smiled at the class as she got everyone's attention. "Okay, is everyone excited to get their instruments?"

Everyone in the room shouted an anxious "Yes!" and Ms. Chase began calling students up to her desk. A girl named Allison was first, and Ms. Chase handed her a shiny saxophone. The girl hurried back to her desk to show all of her friends the instrument. Next, Jason's friend Matt was given a clarinet. He tried blowing into it and the clarinet made a horrible squeak!

Matt looked a little embarrassed, but Ms. Chase told him not to worry. There would be plenty of time for everyone to practice before the show.

One by one, students were called up to Ms. Chase's desk and handed instruments. The trumpet was given to a boy with blond hair, and the trombone was handed to a girl with braids. Pretty soon, even the triangle was gone and it seemed as if there was nothing left for Jason to play!

He wondered whether Ms. Chase had forgotten about him, until he heard his name being called from the front of the room. He walked up to Ms. Chase's desk with a confused look on his face. What instrument would he be given?

Ms. Chase handed him a round instrument with small metal discs on the outer edge.

It was a tambourine, and Ms. Chase explained that it was a very important part of the song that the class would be playing.

Though Ms. Chase seemed pretty excited, Jason was disappointed with his instrument. What was so great about a tambourine? His baby sister could probably play it just as well as anyone else! It didn't seem all that important to Jason.

The next day, Jason still wasn't sure about the tambourine. He stared at the instrument as it sat on his desk in the music room. Ms. Chase was helping the other students set up music stands and tune their instruments. Jason wished that he had been given another instrument. He was sure that even the triangle would be better than the tambourine.

Ms. Chase saw Jason sitting by himself and went over to him. She asked him what was the matter, and Jason told her that he didn't like the tambourine. He said that he didn't think that it was a very important part of the band.

Ms. Chase smiled and said that she understood that the tambourine didn't seem like a very big part. But she explained that a tambourine could really make a song special. While Jason looked at her uncertainly, Ms. Chase had an idea.

She told Jason to join the other students as she stood in front of the band. She asked all of the students to play the song, but she told Jason to wait. Many of the students groaned, because they hadn't had much of a chance to practice the song. Ms. Chase said that it wouldn't matter.

The students followed their sheet music carefully. Many of them made mistakes, but the song didn't sound so bad. When they finished, Ms. Chase asked them to play the song once more, and this time she told Jason to join them.

Jason carefully followed the music and struck the tambourine the way that Ms. Chase had showed him. With the tambourine, the song sounded much livelier! Jason was surprised by how different the song sounded when the tambourine was added.

When they finished, many of the students had smiles on their faces. They thought that their song sounded pretty good, and it would sound even better after they practiced a bit more.

When class was over, Ms. Chase asked Jason what he thought about the song. Jason agreed that the tambourine certainly had made the song sound better.

"See?" she said. "Every part, no matter how small, makes a big sound!"

☇ Questions ☇

1. **Who is the main character in this story?**

    (A) Allison

    (B) Jason

    (C) Ms. Chase

    (D) Matt

 **HINT**

Think about the person who does the most in the story. That person is the main character.

2. **What problem does Jason have with the tambourine?**

    (A) He doesn't think that it's loud enough.

    (B) He doesn't think that it is big enough.

    (C) He doesn't think it's an important instrument.

    (D) He doesn't think he will be able to play it well.

 **HINT**

Think about how Jason feels when he is given the tambourine. Why is he upset with the instrument?

3. **Some words in the story are written in italics to show that**

    Ⓐ these words are Jason's thoughts.

    Ⓑ Jason is feeling very unhappy.

    Ⓒ Ms. Chase is speaking to the class.

    Ⓓ these words are not very important.

HINT

Think about what the words say. How do these words fit into the story? Think about this, and then choose the best answer.

4. **What helps Jason to understand that all the instruments are important parts of the band? Write your answer on the lines below.**

_____

_____

_____

_____

_____

HINT

Think about the end of the story. What happens to make Jason change his mind? Who helps Jason understand that all of the instruments are important?

New Jersey Assessment of Skills and Knowledge

LANGUAGE ARTS LITERACY Grade 4

Section 2: Writing

Chapter 7

Prewriting

How Can Prewriting Help?

Writing is actually a lot like cooking. Think about it. Before you begin to cook, you need to gather all of the ingredients that you will use to make your tasty dish. To write well, you need to gather all of your ideas together before you actually write anything down on paper. This writing before you write is known as **prewriting**. Prewriting helps your ideas to become clear and can even help you to form new ideas. It helps you figure out exactly what you want to say.

During prewriting, you should think about the people who will be reading what you write, or your **audience**. Also, think about why you are writing, or the **purpose** of your writing.

Writing on the NJ ASK

On the NJ ASK, you will be asked to complete two different writing tasks. To do this, you will read writing prompts. A **writing prompt** is a set of directions for your writing. A writing prompt might be a question that you have to answer, or it might be a set of instructions. A writing prompt gives you a topic to write about. It makes you think about a certain subject, and then what you might want to write about that subject.

The test booklet includes blank pages where you **prewrite**, or plan your writing. You won't receive any score for what you write on these blank pages. The blank pages are followed by pages of lines where you will write the final draft of your writing. The final draft of your writing will be scored.

This lesson teaches you about the different writing prompts you will see on the test and how to prewrite in response to a writing prompt. On the NJ ASK, you are given two expository writing prompts. One is based on a familiar topic, and the other is based on a poem.

Simple Prompt

This prompt is based on a familiar topic and asks you to describe, discuss, explain, or analyze some aspect of the topic. You need to draw on your own experience and what you know to develop your ideas into a composition.

Poem Prompt

In the other expository prompt, you are asked to read a poem while your teacher reads it aloud. After you have read the poem, you are asked to think about an idea in the poem and to write a composition based on that idea.

You have 30 minutes to respond to each writing prompt. You should use the first few minutes to prewrite, or make a written plan of what you will write about. You should use the last few minutes to look over your writing and make any changes that you think will make your writing better. You can use a tool called a Writer's Checklist to help you make sure that your writing is as good as it can be. You will see a Writer's Checklist later in this lesson.

Parts of a Writing Prompt

Each writing prompt has the following parts:

• An important topic that gets students to think

• A clear focus

• A clear theme or central idea

• A clear purpose

• A background situation, or context, that helps students think about the topic

To get a good score on the writing section of the test, your writing should do the following:

- Reflect your age and grade level

- Have a clear focus with a clear purpose, or reason that you are writing

- Be supported by details that make sense

- Be clearly organized, with a clear opening and closing

- Use different types of words and different kinds of sentences

- Have a strong stance, or reflect a clear opinion or point

- Show that you understand how to write for a certain audience

Think about these things as you begin to write. Knowing what is expected of your writing before you begin gives you a better idea of what to write.

Ways to Prewrite

Prewriting doesn't have to be perfect. You don't have to use complete sentences or spell everything correctly. You just need to get your ideas written down so that you can look at them and decide which ones you will use in your writing. There are many different ways to prewrite. You can make a list, form an idea web, or use another kind of graphic organizer. You will learn how to do this in the prompt practice sections of this lesson.

How to Prewrite for a Simple Prompt

On the NJ ASK, you are asked to write a composition about something with which you are familiar. It could be a favorite thing or something you like to do. The important thing to remember is that you will be writing about a topic that you know a lot about. You need to draw on your own experience to explain why something is your favorite thing or why you enjoy doing a specific thing.

When you take the test, you will see a Writer's Checklist. The Writer's Checklist on the NJ ASK helps you make sure you stay on track while you write. It tells you what to focus on to help you get a better score.

Here is an example of the Writer's Checklist you will see on the NJ ASK test. The boldface sentences have to do with prewriting.

Writer's Checklist

Remember to

- ❑ **Keep the central idea or topic in mind.**

- ❑ **Keep your audience in mind.**

- ❑ Support your ideas with details, explanations, and examples.

- ❑ State your ideas in a clear sequence.

- ❑ Include an opening and a closing.

- ❑ Use a variety of words and vary your sentence structure.

- ❑ State your opinion or conclusion clearly.

- ❑ Capitalize, spell, and use punctuation correctly.

- ❑ Write neatly.

A simple prompt on the NJ ASK will be like the one on the opposite page.

Sample Writing Task

Most people have a favorite way to spend a day. Some people like to do things outside, while others like to do indoor activities. What is your favorite way to spend a day?

Write a composition describing how you would like to spend your day. Explain why this activity is special to you.

To begin prewriting, you can make a list of the ways you would like to spend a day. Think about the things you like to do that are the most fun and make a list. Your list might look like this:

Playing sports such as baseball and soccer

Rollerblading at the park

Biking with my family

Going on a trip to the zoo

Going to an amusement park

Now choose the best idea on your list to write about. What idea is most special to you? Which idea can you write about using the most detail? Which idea will your audience find most interesting?

Once you've selected your topic, you will need to come up with some details about it. On the next page you will find a way to organize the details you want to include in your composition.

Another way to prewrite is by making a web or other **graphic organizer**. A graphic organizer is a picture summary of information. Let's say you decide to write about a day at an amusement park. You can put the details of what you like to do at an amusement park in a graphic organizer. Your graphic organizer might look like this:

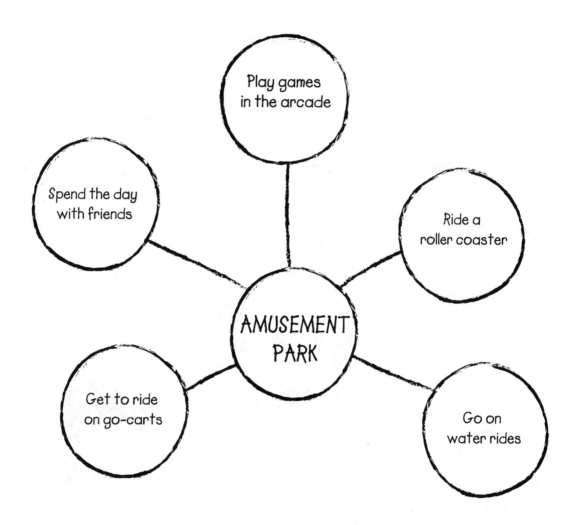

These are just a couple of ways to prewrite. You will get more practice prewriting later in this lesson. After you learn many different ways to prewrite, you can decide which way works best for you.

How to Prewrite for a Poem Prompt

On the NJ ASK, you will also read a poem while your teacher reads it aloud. Then you will be asked to write a composition based on an idea in the poem. You will also be given a Writer's Checklist to help you write a good composition about that idea.

A poem prompt on the NJ ASK will look like this:

Sample Writing Task

Block City

by Robert Louis Stevenson

What are you able to build with your blocks?
Castles and palaces, temples and docks.
Rain may keep raining, and others go roam,
But I can be happy and building at home.

Let the sofa be mountains, the carpet be sea,
There I'll establish a city for me:
A kirk and a mill and a palace beside,
And a harbour as well where my vessels may ride.

Great is the palace with pillar and wall,
A sort of a tower on the top of it all,
And steps coming down in an orderly way
To where my toy vessels lie safe in the bay.

This one is sailing and that one is moored:
Hark to the song of the sailors aboard!
And see, on the steps of my palace, the kings
Coming and going with presents and things!

Now I have done with it, down let it go!
All in a moment the town is laid low.
Block upon block lying scattered and free,
What is there left of my town by the sea?

Yet as I saw it, I see it again,
The kirk and the palace, the ships and the men,
And as long as I live and where'er I may be,
I'll always remember my town by the sea.

In "Block City," the poet writes about a city that he built from blocks. The poet used his imagination to pretend that his city was a beautiful town by the sea, and he said that he will always remember this town. At some time or another, you have probably thought about the place where you would like to live when you grow up. Write a composition about the place where you want to live when you get older.

In your composition, be sure to do the following:

• **Describe the place where you want to live**

• **Explain why you want to live there**

• **Tell how this place is like or different from the place where you live now**

● ● ●

So, that is what a poem prompt looks like. Now, think about the place where you want to live when you get older. Then start prewriting. If you choose to write a list, it may look something like this:

Where I want to live:

Different from the city where I live now

Wide open spaces

Fresh, clean air

Small neighborhood

Friendly people

Calm, relaxed atmosphere

Now choose the best ideas on your list to write about. What ideas will give your audience the best image of the place where you want to live? Which ideas can you write about using the most details? Which ideas will your audience find to be the most interesting?

Creating a graphic organizer like the one below will help you when you are ready to write your composition.

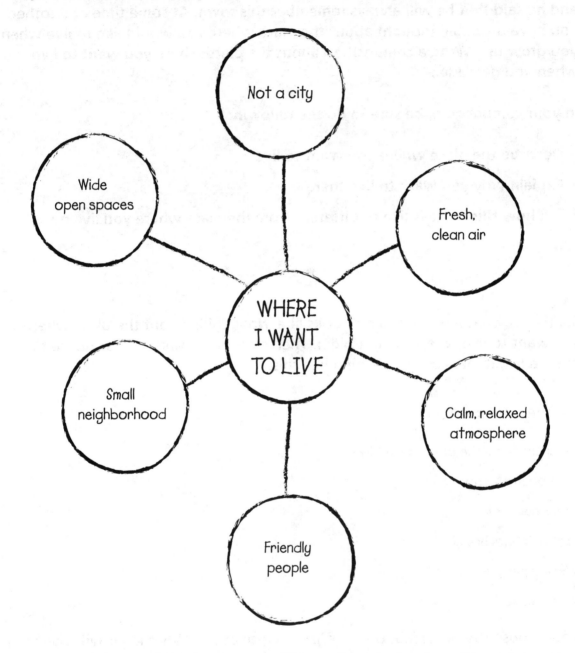

In the next chapter of this book, you will learn how to begin writing your composition.

Chapter 8

Drafting and Revising

In Chapter 7, you learned about prewriting. You learned that doing some prewriting will help you when you begin to write. In this chapter, you will learn how to draft your composition. When you draft your composition, you begin writing it.

Remember the checklist you saw in the last chapter? It's printed again below. But this time, the sentences that are boldface have to do with drafting.

Writer's Checklist

Remember these tips:

- ❑ Keep the central idea or topic in mind.
- ❑ Keep your audience in mind.
- ❑ **Support your ideas with details, explanations, and examples.**
- ❑ **State your ideas in a clear sequence.**
- ❑ **Include an opening and a closing.**
- ❑ **Use a variety of words and vary your sentence structure.**
- ❑ **State your opinion or conclusion clearly.**
- ❑ Capitalize, spell, and use punctuation correctly.
- ❑ Write neatly.

Beginning, Middle, and End

Your composition should have three paragraphs: a beginning, middle, and end. The first paragraph is an introduction. An **introduction** is a beginning. It should tell what your composition is about. It should *name* your topic. For example, in the composition about a day at an amusement park, you might write:

My favorite way to spend the day is going to an amusement park.

This sentence tells what your composition is about. After this sentence you can *explain* why going to an amusement park is your favorite way to spend the day.

A good way to remember what to write in your first paragraph is that it should *name and explain*.

Use a Variety of Words

When you write, you should use a variety of words and sentences. The word "variety" simply means "different kinds." Read the sentences below:

Amusement parks are special places to me. Amusement parks have water rides. Amusement parks have roller coasters. Amusement parks have go-cart rides.

Did you enjoy reading those sentences? No! They're very short. They also use the words "Amusement parks" too often.

Now read these sentences:

Amusement parks are special places to me. I love the water rides and can never get enough of the roller coasters. But my favorite ride is the go-carts.

Much better!

Details

In the second paragraph, the middle, you will need to answer this question: ***Why is it important to me?*** When you write your composition, be sure you include enough details to make your point. A detail can be anything that supports your main idea. It can be an example or an explanation.

If you were writing in response to the simple prompt in the last chapter, you would need details to show why going to an amusement park is your favorite way to spend the day. If you don't include details, your reader might not understand what makes it so special. The second paragraph of your composition must give specific reasons why a day at the amusement park is important to you.

Opinions and Conclusions

In the third paragraph, the end, you will need to answer this question: ***why is it great?*** You will tell the reader why what you have chosen to write about is great. This is your opinion. An **opinion** is what you think about something. For example, when writing about amusement parks, you might say:

An amusement park is a place where a kid can have the best time in the world.

Your **conclusion** is a statement that ends your composition. You sum up all your thoughts and details from the first two paragraphs. You might also want to end with a question for your reader. For example:

I love spending the day at an amusement park. Wouldn't you want to spend a day is at an amusement park too?

When you express your opinions or write a conclusion on the NJ ASK, be sure to include enough details to show the reader why you think the way that you do.

How to Draft for a Simple Prompt

Remember the simple prompt from Chapter 7? It's printed again here along with the list of details and graphic organizer.

> **Most people have a favorite way to spend a day. Some people like to do things outside, while others like to do indoor activities. What is your favorite way to spend a day?**
>
> **Write a composition describing how you would like to spend your day. Explain why this activity is special to you.**

Details

1. Get to ride on go-carts

2. Spend the day with friends

3. Play games in the arcade

4. Ride a roller coaster

5. Go on water rides

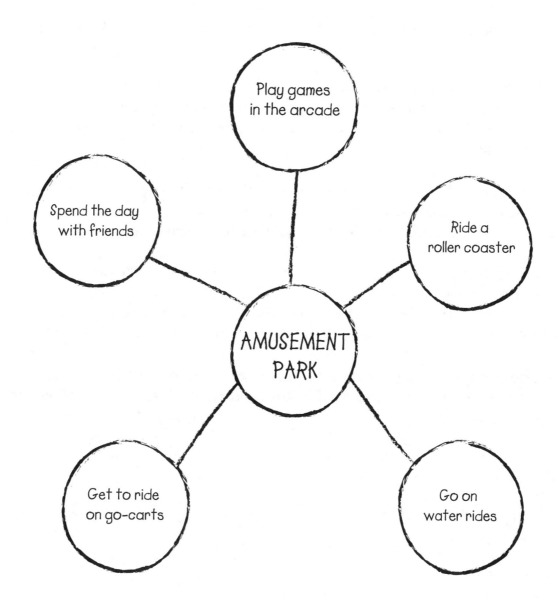

Now it's time to get writing. The following draft is a good draft. It's not perfect! But it's getting there.

My favorite way to spend the day is going to an amusement park. Amusement parks are special places to me. I love the water rides and can never get enough of the roller coasters. I especially enjoy going to an amusement park with my Friends. We never stop laughing.

My favorite ride is the go-carts. Ever since I was a little child. I have wanted to drive a car. Since I am still not old enough to drive, go-carts are the next best thing. I pretend I am driving a real car every time I go for a ride it feels great!

An amusement park is a place where a kid can have the best time in the world. You can go on rides that are fun and scarey. You can cool off if it is hot outside. An amusement park has something everyone enjoys. I love spending the day at an amusement park. Wouldn't you want to spend a day is at an amusement park too?

What do you think? It's a good start, isn't it? Did you see any errors in the composition? There are a few. We'll fix these errors in a later section, "Revising."

How to Write a Draft for a Poem Prompt

In chapter 7, you read a poem. You learned that for one of the writing tasks on the NJ ASK, you would have to write a response to this poem. Here are the writing task, poem, and the prewriting we did in chapter 7.

Sample Writing Task

In "Block City," the poet writes about a city that he built from blocks. The poet used his imagination to pretend that his city was a beautiful town by the sea, and he said that he will always remember this town. At some time or another, you have probably thought about the place where you would like to live when you grow up. Write a composition about the place where you want to live when you get older.

In your composition, be sure to

- Describe the place where you want to live

- Explain why you want to live there

- Tell how this place is alike or different from the place where you live now

Block City

by Robert Louis Stevenson

What are you able to build with your blocks?
Castles and palaces, temples and docks.
Rain may keep raining, and others go roam,
But I can be happy and building at home.

Let the sofa be mountains, the carpet be sea,
There I'll establish a city for me:
A kirk and a mill and a palace beside,
And a harbour as well where my vessels may ride.

Great is the palace with pillar and wall,
A sort of a tower on the top of it all,
And steps coming down in an orderly way
To where my toy vessels lie safe in the bay.

This one is sailing and that one is moored:
Hark to the song of the sailors aboard!
And see, on the steps of my palace, the kings
Coming and going with presents and things!

Now I have done with it, down let it go!
All in a moment the town is laid low.
Block upon block lying scattered and free,
What is there left of my town by the sea?

Yet as I saw it, I see it again,
The kirk and the palace, the ships and the men,
And as long as I live and where'er I may be,
I'll always remember my town by the sea.

Where I want to live:

Different from the city where I live now

Wide, open spaces

Fresh, clean air

Small neighborhood

Friendly people

Calm, relaxed atmosphere

Creating a graphic organizer like the one below will help you when you are ready to write your composition.

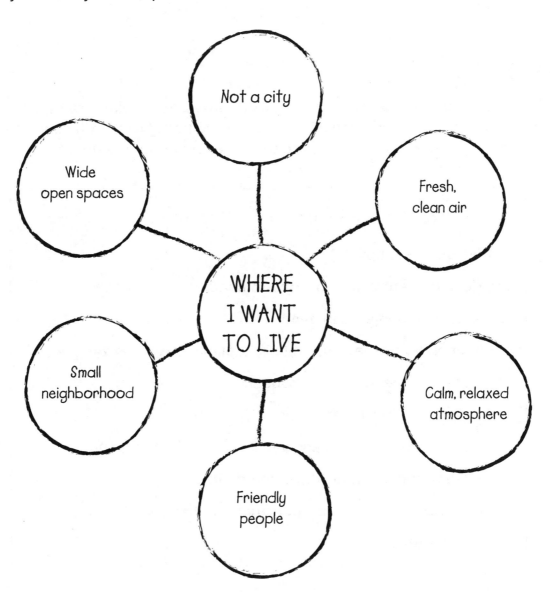

When I grow up, I want to live in the country I want to live in a house with a huge yard and a lot of wide, open spaces. My house will be surrounded by trees and grass. The air will be fresh and clean. I want to live in a small neighborhood. Filled with lots of friendly people that I know by name. I want to feel calm and relaxed all the time.

I want to live in a place like this because I have always lived in the city. In the city, there are so many people that you rarely see the same ones each day. Also, people are always out and about. It seems like they are always busy and and never stop to rest and relax. The streets are filled with loud, smelly cars. The sidewalks are lined with huge buildings. The only trees and grass are in the park across town. I like the city. But I think that I would like living a quiet life in the country more.

What do you think of this composition? It is a good first draft. Do you see some errors? We'll fix these errors in the next section.

Revising

When you revise your composition, you fix mistakes. You make sure that your composition is as good as it can be. Look at the Writer's Checklist below. The last two sentences are boldface. These sentences are about revising.

Writer's Checklist

Remember these tips:

- ❏ Keep the central idea or topic in mind.
- ❏ Keep your audience in mind.
- ❏ Support your ideas with details, explanations, and examples.
- ❏ State your ideas in a clear sequence.
- ❏ Include an opening and a closing.
- ❏ Use a variety of words and vary your sentence structure.
- ❏ State your opinion or conclusion clearly.
- ❏ **Capitalize, spell, and use punctuation correctly.**
- ❏ **Write neatly.**

When you revise your composition, check to make sure that you have a capital letter at the beginning of each sentence. Street names and people's names should be capitalized. However, seasons of the year (spring, summer, fall, and winter) are not capitalized. Also check to make sure that you have spelled all of your words correctly. Check that each of your sentences has a period, an exclamation point, or a question mark after it. Make sure that you don't run two sentences into one and that each sentence in your composition is a complete sentence and not just part of a sentence.

Notice the revisions in the first composition we wrote together.

My favorite way to spend the day is going to an amusement park. Amusement parks are special places to me. I love the water rides and can never get enough of the roller coasters. I especially enjoy going to an amusement park with my fFriends. We never stop laughing.

My favorite ride is the go-carts. Ever since I was a little child, I have wanted to drive a car. Since I am still not old enough to drive, go-carts are the next best thing. I pretend I am driving a real car every time I go for a ride. Itt feels great!

An amusement park is a place where a kid can have the best time in the world. You can go on rides that are fun and scarey scary. You can cool off if it is hot outside. An amusement park has something everyone enjoys. I love spending the day at an amusement park. Wouldn't you want to spend a day is at an amusement park too?

Now let's look at the revisions on the second essay.

When I grow up, I want to live in the country. I want to live in a house with a huge yard and a lot of wide, open spaces. My house will be surrounded by trees and grass. The air will be fresh and clean. I want to live in a small neighborhood. Filled with lots of friendly people that I know by name. I want to feel calm and relaxed all the time.

I want to live in a place like this because I have always lived in the city. In the city, there are so many people that you rarely see the same ones each day. Also, people are always out and about. It seems like they are always busy and and never stop to rest and relax. The streets are filled with loud, smelly cars. The sidewalks are lined with huge buildings. The only trees and grass are in the park across town. I like the city, but I think that I would like living a quiet life in the country more.

New Jersey Assessment of Skills and Knowledge

LANGUAGE ARTS LITERACY Grade 4

Practice Test 1

Directions to the Student

Read the question on page 122. Write a composition about something new you tried to do recently.

You may take notes, create a web, or do other prewriting work in the space provided on pages 123 and 124. Then write your composition on the lines provided on pages 125 and 126.

Here is a checklist for you to follow to help you do your best writing. Please read it silently as I read it aloud to you.

Writer's Checklist

Remember to

❑ Keep the central idea or topic in mind.

❑ Keep your audience in mind.

❑ Support your ideas with details, explanations, and examples.

❑ State your ideas in a clear sequence.

❑ Include an opening and a closing.

❑ Use a variety of words and vary your sentence structure.

❑ State your opinion or conclusion clearly.

❑ Capitalize, spell, and use punctuation correctly.

❑ Write neatly.

After you write your composition, read what you have written. Use the checklist to make certain that your writing is the best it can be.

Writing Task 1

What is something new you have tried recently? Write a composition about what you tried and how you felt when you tried it.

In your composition, be sure to

- Describe what you tried to do

- Tell why you tried to do it

- Explain how you felt before you tried it

- Explain how you felt after you tried it

- Tell what you learned from your experience.

WRITING TASK 1 – PREWRITING SPACE
Use the space below and on page 124 to plan your writing.

WRITING TASK 1 – PREWRITING SPACE (continued)

Remember — your story must be written on the lines on pages
125 and 126 ONLY.

WRITING TASK 1

Something new I tried recently was riding my bike. The reason I tried to do it was becuse the weather started to get warmer so then I said to my self I'm gonna get some fresh air so I asked my dad if I could ride my bike. Before I got on my bike I was pretty scared because I haven't rode it in a while. When I finished riding my bike I felt so good because I got fresh air, exercise, and got wind blowing in my face. I leared that trying something new is always fun.

WRITING TASK 1 (continued)

_____

_____

_____

_____

_____

_____

_____

_____

_____

_____

_____

_____

_____

_____

_____

If you have time, you may review your work in this section only.

STOP

DO NOT GO ON
UNTIL YOU ARE
TOLD TO DO SO.

Directions to the Student

Now you will read a story and answer the questions that follow.

Some questions will be multiple-choice; others will be open-ended.

1. You may look back at the reading passage as often as you want.

2. Read each question carefully and think about the answer.

3. For each multiple-choice question, select the best answer and fill in the circle next to your choice. Make sure you fill in the correct circle.

4. If you do not know the answer to a question, go on to the next question. You may come back to the skipped question later if you have time.

One More Chance . . .

Ryan Trevor knocked the mud from his shoes with the baseball bat and stepped up to home plate. *Remember, eye on the ball,* he said to himself.

The first ball flew by Ryan. He did not have the chance to move before hearing the smack in the catcher's mitt.

"Strike one!" yelled the umpire.

Ryan took a deep breath and got ready for the next pitch. *Eye on the ball.*

The Giants' pitcher wound up and fired another ball across home plate. Ryan swung the bat with all his might but connected with nothing but air.

"Strike two!" the umpire yelled.

It was the end of the last inning. The Giants were up eight to seven over Ryan's team, the Tigers. Becky Riley and Tom Fields were both on base. If Ryan could somehow manage to hit a double, he could send both of them home and the Tigers would win the game. Problem was, the Tigers had two outs and Ryan already had two strikes against him. The fact that he had not had a hit or made it to first base all season weighed on his mind. If he struck out now, his team would lose not only the game but also their chance to go to the playoffs.

How did I get myself into this mess? Ryan thought.

It was a chilly Saturday in February when Ryan's best friend, Matt Richards, called to tell Ryan about Little League sign-ups. Ryan did not play baseball all that often, but he was pretty good at football. He thought that after a few practices he would certainly get the hang of one of America's favorite games. He began to discover just how wrong he was at his first practice.

Coach Davis stood on the mound ready to pitch.

"You will each get the chance to hit three baseballs," said Coach Davis. "After all, if you get three strikes in a game, you are out."

Ryan watched as everyone on his team stepped up to the plate and got at least one hit. Then it was Ryan's turn.

Foomp! The first baseball sailed toward Ryan, who swung the bat wildly and missed. Strike one.

"Keep your eye on the ball, Ryan!" yelled Matt from the dugout. The second ball flew toward him. Ryan watched it so closely that he forgot to swing his bat. Strike two.

"All right, Ryan, last one. Make it count!" shouted Coach Davis.

Ryan crouched down, dug his toe in the dirt, and got ready. Foomp! He watched the ball make its approach, but just as he was about to swing, it walloped him right in the elbow. Strike three.

Ryan grabbed his arm, jumping up and down in pain. He spent the rest of the practice warming the bench. *Off to a great start,* he thought.

The rest of the season had not gone much better than the first practice. When it was his turn to bat, all the players on team would cross their fingers in the hope that he would hit the ball. Their wishes never came true.

Now the whole season came down to this one moment. Ryan had one more chance to make up for all his strikeouts. He swallowed a big lump in his throat. *This is it, Ryan.*

Ryan watched as the Giants' pitcher, his face as blank as an empty desktop, stepped forward and fired the ball in Ryan's direction.

Ryan swung hard.

"Strike three! You are outta there!" yelled the umpire.

Ryan dropped the bat by his feet and watched as the Giants celebrated their victory. Without looking at his teammates, Ryan grabbed his mitt from the bench in the dugout and started toward the car. He was looking around for his mother when she suddenly came up behind him and began gently shaking his shoulders.

"Ryan, time to wake up," said Mrs. Trevor. "Rise and shine."

Ryan opened his eyes just enough to peer at his mother out from under his tangled blanket. Bright sunlight streamed through his bedroom windows.

"We have to hurry and get to the ball field for the game," Ryan's mother said.

"The game?" Ryan asked, rubbing the sleep out of his eyes and sitting straight up. "You mean I still have one more chance?"

"One more chance for what?" asked Mrs. Trevor.

"Never mind," said Ryan. He jumped out of bed to grab his crisp, clean uniform. He caught a glimpse of himself in the mirror and thought with a smile, *one more chance!*

1. **What is the purpose of the flashback used in the story?**

   Ⓐ to describe Ryan's friendship with Matt Richards

   Ⓑ to give information about the people on Ryan's team

   Ⓒ to explain how Ryan learned to play baseball

   Ⓓ to show that Ryan is not a very good baseball player

2. **What is a theme of "One More Chance"?**

   Ⓐ Fight for what you believe in.

   Ⓑ It is better to tell the truth than to lie.

   Ⓒ Never stop believing in yourself.

   Ⓓ Treat others the way you want to be treated.

3. **What does the word "walloped" mean in the following sentence: "He watched the ball make its approach, but just as he was about to swing, it walloped him right in the elbow"?**

   Ⓐ slid

   Ⓑ hit

   Ⓒ rolled

   Ⓓ bounced

4. **How does Ryan probably feel when he realizes that he has struck out?**

   Ⓐ relaxed

   Ⓑ anxious

   Ⓒ troubled

   Ⓓ scared

5. **What does the expression "his face as blank as an empty desktop" tell you about the Giants' pitcher?**

   Ⓐ He is not a very interesting person.

   Ⓑ He is wondering if his team will win.

   Ⓒ He is usually not very serious about baseball.

   Ⓓ He is thinking very hard about what he is doing.

6. **What would probably happen if Ryan got a hit in the game?**

   Ⓐ His coach would make him team captain.

   Ⓑ His teammates would cheer with excitement.

   Ⓒ His mother would let him sleep in for a change.

   Ⓓ His friend Matt would score a run to win the championship.

7. Why does the author use italics in the story?

Ⓐ to show that Ryan's teammates are upset

Ⓑ to indicate that Ryan is thinking

Ⓒ to show that something happened in the past

Ⓓ to highlight that the umpire is yelling

8. At the end of the story, why does Ryan seem so puzzled?

Ⓐ He does not realize that he was dreaming about baseball.

Ⓑ He does not want his team to be in the baseball playoffs.

Ⓒ He does not understand why he is such a bad baseball player.

Ⓓ He does not want to let his baseball team down again.

9. How might this story help a reader?

Ⓐ by inspiring the reader to always keep trying

Ⓑ by teaching the reader the rules of baseball

Ⓒ by showing the reader how to treat other people

Ⓓ by making the reader want to play different sports

For the open-ended questions on the next page, remember to

- Focus your response on the question asked.
- Answer all parts of the question.
- Give a complete explanation.
- Use specific information from the story.

10. Ryan is happy to have "one more chance" at the end of the story. Explain what this shows about Ryan.

Use information from the story to support your response.

Write your answer on the lines below.

_____

_____

_____

_____

_____

_____

_____

_____

_____

_____

_____

_____

_____

_____

_____

_____

If you have time, you may review your work in this section only.

STOP

DO NOT GO ON
UNTIL YOU ARE
TOLD TO DO SO.

Directions: Read the article and answer the questions that follow.

To Sleep, Perhaps to Dream

"Get up, sleepyhead!" Children all around the world hear this cry every morning. In this day and age, we all have so much to do that sleep can seem like a waste of time. But is it a good idea to sleep less in order to get more done? No! Sleep is as important to the brain and body as food. Without enough sleep, people are not able to think clearly and are too tired to get things done. Adults need about eight hours of sleep a night to function well during the day. Children need 10 to 12 hours of sleep a night.

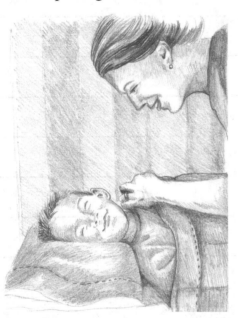

Why do we sleep?

We do not know for sure what sleep is for, but most scientists agree that we sleep for several different reasons.

To recover from activity

Sleep helps the body rest and recover from a busy day. The more active people or animals are during the day, the deeper they sleep at night.

To process information

Have you ever had a dream that made you feel funny when you woke up? Your brain might have been using this dream to understand or remember something that happened when you were awake. It is possible that dreams, even strange ones, help people process information and preserve memories.

To protect from harm

Studies show that sleep may help protect people and animals from germs. Sleep seems to make the immune system stronger and help the body fight infection. During sleep, blood cells that attack germs increase in number. This may explain why people and animals get sleepy when they do get sick.

Good night, sleep tight

No matter what the reason for sleep, getting a good night of it can make your brain function better the next day. A few simple steps can help you have a good night's sleep:

1. Do not watch TV or read the Internet right before you go to bed. The light from the screen can stimulate your brain and keep you awake.

2. Do not eat sweet foods or drink soda right before you go to bed. Sugar can keep you awake.

3. Sleep in a dark room. Even the light from a clock can trick your brain into staying partly awake.

4. Make your bed and your room as comfortable as possible. Open a window for fresh air, if you wish, and be sure you have a comfortable pillow and plenty of cozy blankets.

5. Be sure to get at least 10 hours of sleep a night. You will benefit most from sound slumber. Getting too much or too little sleep can affect its quality.

Fun Facts about Animal Sleep

• When birds migrate, they can stay awake for days as they fly to their new homes.

• Brown bats sleep almost 20 hours a day.

• Giraffes sleep only about 2 hours a day.

• Elephants sleep standing up during light sleep and lying down during deep sleep.

• Sea otters float on their backs to sleep, and otter babies sleep on their mothers' stomachs.

• Orangutans sleep in nests in trees with all their fingers and toes wrapped around branches.

• Dolphins sleep with only one half of their brains at a time. One half sleeps while the other half is awake.

11. **What does the word "recover" mean in the following sentence: "Sleep helps the body rest and recover from a busy day"?**

Ⓐ put on top again

Ⓑ figure things out

● get back to normal

Ⓓ get things done

12. **Dreams help people**

Ⓐ get enough sleep.

Ⓑ learn how to fight germs.

Ⓒ relate better to animals.

● understand and remember events.

13. **Why do you probably sleep more deeply on some nights than others?**

● You sleep more deeply when you are more active during the day.

Ⓑ You sleep more deeply when you sleep for more hours per night.

Ⓒ You sleep more deeply when the clock on your bedside table is on.

Ⓓ You sleep more deeply when people keep trying to wake you up.

14. **Read this sentence from the article.**

"Have you ever had a dream that made you feel funny when you woke up?"

What does "funny" mean in this sentence?

Ⓐ strange

Ⓑ amused

Ⓒ tired

Ⓓ interested

15. **Watching TV right before bed will**

Ⓐ make you hungry for sweet treats.

Ⓑ cause you to have long dreams.

Ⓒ cause you need to fresh air.

Ⓓ make it hard for you to go to sleep.

16. **Why does the author start the article with an exclamation?**

Ⓐ to make sure the reader is awake and paying attention

Ⓑ to show that the article is discussing an important problem

Ⓒ to give an example of something that children like to hear

Ⓓ to highlight that all people everywhere sleep

17. **What is the main idea of "To Sleep, Perhaps to Dream"?**

Ⓐ Be sure to get the same amount of sleep every night of the week.

Ⓑ Different animals have unusual and interesting sleep habits.

Ⓒ Both people and animals need plenty of sleep to do things well.

Ⓓ Some behavior can make falling asleep difficult.

18. **Why do dolphins most likely sleep with one half of their brain at a time?**

Ⓐ Only one side of their brain is tired.

Ⓑ Their brains are not fully formed.

Ⓒ They need to make more blood cells.

Ⓓ They want to be alert in case of danger.

19. **Which of these would probably be the best place for you to get a good night's sleep?**

Ⓐ on the couch in front of the television

Ⓑ in a comfortable bed under the covers

Ⓒ in a cushioned chair by a computer

Ⓓ surrounded by light in a cozy bed

For the open-ended questions on the next page, remember to

- Focus your response on the question asked.
- Answer all parts of the question.
- Give a complete explanation.
- Use specific information from the story.

TURN TO THE NEXT PAGE. ▶

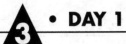
20. **What if you had a hard time sleeping one night and ended up sleeping for only five hours? Explain what problems you might have the next day. Use examples from the article to support your answer.**

Write your answer on the lines below.

_____

_____

_____

_____

_____

_____

_____

_____

_____

_____

_____

_____

_____

_____

If you have time, you may review your work in this section only.

STOP

CLOSE YOUR BOOK.

Directions to the Student

Read the poem "Young Night-Thought" to yourself while I read it aloud to you. Afterward, you will do a writing task. The poem may give you ideas for your writing.

Young Night-Thought

by Robert Louis Stevenson

All night long and every night,
When my mama puts out the light,
I see the people marching by,
As plain as day before my eye.

Armies and emperors and kings,
All carrying different kinds of things,
And marching in so grand a way,
You never saw the like by day.

So fine a show was never seen
At the great circus on the green;
For every kind of beast and man
Is marching in that caravan.

At first they move a little slow,
But still the faster on they go,
And still beside me close I keep
Until we reach the town of Sleep.

TURN TO THE NEXT PAGE.

Writing Task 2

In "Young Night-Thought," the poet Robert Louis Stevenson writes about the things a child is thinking and dreaming as he or she drifts off to sleep. At one time or another, most of us have had a strange or interesting dream while we were sleeping. Write a composition about a strange or interesting dream that you have had.

In your composition, be sure to

- **Describe what it is that happened to you in your dream.**
- **Give details about what your dream world was like.**
- **Explain whether or not you would visit this dream world if it were a real place.**

You may take notes, create a web, or do other prewriting work in the space provided on pages 145 and 146. Then write your composition on the lines provided on pages 147 and 148.

Here is a checklist for you to follow to help you do your best writing. Please read it silently as I read it aloud to you.

Writer's Checklist

Remember to

❑ Keep the central idea or topic in mind.

❑ Keep your audience in mind.

❑ Support your ideas with details, explanations, and examples.

❑ State your ideas in a clear sequence.

❑ Include an opening and a closing.

❑ Use a variety of words and vary your sentence structure.

❑ State your opinion or conclusion clearly.

❑ Capitalize, spell, and use punctuation correctly.

❑ Write neatly.

After you write your composition, read what you have written. Use the checklist to make certain that your writing is the best it can be.

 TURN TO THE NEXT PAGE.

WRITING TASK 2 – PREWRITING SPACE
Use the space below and on page 146 to plan your writing.

TURN TO THE NEXT PAGE.

WRITING TASK 2 – PREWRITING SPACE (continued)

Remember — your story must be written on the lines on pages
147 and 148 ONLY.

WRITING TASK 2

When I was sleeping I had a dream about a Kangaroo putting me in its pouch. It was pretty strange but then again it was fun hopping around to other places. The wrold I was in wasn't Earth cause I could see earth from where I was standing. I thought to my self and said if Venus is in fron't of earth and I'm behid earth I have to be Mars. The planet was all red with these green creatures that scared the pee out of me. The wether was not to hot but it was pretty cool. Maby when I grow up I can visit Mars.

WRITING TASK 2 (continued)

_____

_____

_____

_____

_____

_____

_____

_____

_____

_____

_____

_____

_____

_____

_____

_____

If you have time, you may review your work in this section only.

DO NOT GO ON
UNTIL YOU ARE
TOLD TO DO SO.

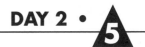

Directions to the Student

In the following section, you will read a passage and answer the questions that follow.

Some questions will be multiple-choice; others will be open-ended.

1. You may look back at the reading passage as often as you want.

2. Read each question carefully and think about the answer.

3. For each multiple-choice question, select the best answer and fill in the circle next to your choice. Make sure you fill in the correct circle.

4. If you do not know the answer to a question, go on to the next question. You may come back to the skipped question later if you have time.

Directions: Read the article and answer the questions that follow.

Local girl on a mission to save the planet

WEEHAWKEN, N.J. – Six months ago, 10-year-old Amanda Carlisle learned that the dripping faucet in the kitchen of her home was causing a large amount of water to be wasted each year. Since then, Amanda has tried hard to save water and to reduce waste. She now spends much of her free time helping to protect the environment. Just last week, Amanda and her father spent the day cleaning up litter by the side of the road.

"It is upsetting to see how much garbage people just throw on the street," said Amanda. "We only have one planet. What are we going to do if we just keep filling it with garbage?"

Amanda said that she had not always been so worried about saving water and protecting the environment. She often spent summer days running through the sprinkler and tossing water balloons around the yard. However, all of that changed when she learned about saving water in science class. Amanda was given an assignment to check her house for dripping faucets. It did not take long for her to find one.

"We figured out that the faucet in my kitchen was dripping one time every second. We put a water glass under it and were surprised at how fast it filled up," Amanda said.

Amanda's class added up how much water the dripping faucet wasted in one year.

"More than 2,000 gallons," said Amanda. "That's about 400 bathtubs full! I couldn't believe how much was wasted. It made me feel so bad."

By that evening, Amanda was on her father's case to fix the dripping faucet. "I fixed it that very night," he said.

After that, Amanda did everything she could to save water and energy. She checked all of the other faucets in the house for leaks. She took shorter showers. Now she turns the water off when she brushes her teeth. She turns off the lights every time she leaves the room. She also polices her family to make sure they do the same.

"It's not that hard to conserve if you just give it a little bit of thought," said Amanda. "When I help my mom with the dishes, we fill one side of the sink with soap and water and the other side with clean water. Mom washes dishes in the soap and water, and I rinse them in the clean water. That way we do not have to run the water in between washing each dish. And when we are done, we use the rinse water to water our plants. Nothing is wasted. It's so simple."

The Carlisle family also recycles everything they can at home. Several bins in their

garage have been set aside to hold paper, metal cans, bottles, and cardboard. Once a week, the family brings everything in to the recycling center.

The Carlisle family tries to conserve and recycle outside the home, too. At school, Amanda and her brother always use both sides of a sheet of paper. They pack their lunches in lunch boxes instead of paper bags. They bring cloth napkins instead of using paper ones.

"Amanda has helped us all learn to conserve," said Mr. Carlisle. "Both my wife and I recycle cardboard, paper and cans at work. And when we go to the grocery store, we take cloth bags with us instead of using paper or plastic bags. Our whole family works a few hours each Saturday to pick up litter along the roads."

Amanda's family agrees that saving the world can sometimes be hard work. "But we do want to make a difference," Amanda added. "We have to take care of our planet now, or it will not be here for us to take care of later."

TURN TO THE NEXT PAGE.

21. The purpose of the first paragraph is to

    Ⓐ introduce how Amanda Carlisle is trying to help the planet.

    Ⓑ give a summary of the different ways to save water in your home.

    Ⓒ explain the ways in which Amanda Carlisle once wasted water.

    Ⓓ explain why you should clean up litter alongside the road.

22. What does the word "conserve" mean in the following sentence:
"'It's not that hard to conserve if you just give it a little bit of thought,'
said Amanda"?

    Ⓐ look

    Ⓑ clean

    Ⓒ save

    Ⓓ change

23. Amanda's father fixed the dripping faucet quickly because

    Ⓐ he was worried about water leaking on the floor.

    Ⓑ his daughter explained that the faucet was wasting water.

    Ⓒ the noise of the dripping water was keeping him awake all night.

    Ⓓ the water kept filling the bathtub dangerously full.

24. **When did Amanda Carlisle learn that the dripping faucet in her kitchen was wasting water?**

Ⓐ while helping to clean up the Earth

Ⓑ while playing a game with her brother

Ⓒ while watching her sink get fixed

● while doing homework for school

25. **What does the word "reduce" mean in the first paragraph of the article?**

● improve

Ⓑ measure

Ⓒ lower

Ⓓ deliver

26. **Why does Amanda bring her lunch to school in a lunch box?**

● Paper bags are a waste of paper.

Ⓑ Her parents use all the cloth bags for shopping.

Ⓒ All the other kids bring lunch boxes.

Ⓓ She can use it for collecting litter after school.

TURN TO THE NEXT PAGE. ➡

27. Read this sentence from the last paragraph of the article.

"Amanda's family agrees that saving the world can sometimes be hard work.

What do they mean?

Ⓐ Saving the world can sometimes seem like a waste of time.

Ⓑ It can sometimes take time and effort to reduce waste and recycle.

Ⓒ Solving all the problems in the world is not an easy task.

Ⓓ Too much hard work can make life difficult at home.

28. The author uses quotations from Amanda and her father in the article to

Ⓐ show that they are friendly people who like to explain things.

Ⓑ make the article seem more like a fictional short story.

Ⓒ let them tell in their own words how they feel about conserving.

Ⓓ prove that the Carlisle family are real people.

29. What would Amanda probably say to a classmate who dropped his empty granola bar wrapper on the ground?

Ⓐ She would look for her teacher and tell what happened.

Ⓑ She would say nothing but come back later to pick up the wrapper.

Ⓒ She would explain to him that they should not bring granola bars to school.

Ⓓ She would ask him to pick it up and remind him to take better care of the environment.

For the open-ended questions on the next page, remember to

- Focus your response on the question asked.

- Answer all parts of the question.

- Give a complete explanation.

- Use specific information from the story.

30. **Think about what you can do to reduce waste in your own life. Pick something that you do everyday that is wasteful. What can you do to make this activity less wasteful? Use information from the article to support your response. Write your answer on the lines below.**

Something I do in my every day life that is wasteful is asking for food then only taking one bite. The thing I can make this activity better is by getting a little at a time so I don't waste the food. The reason why this activity is wasteful is because you pay for it then you don't eat it and you throw away all of it wich is pretty much throwing away money.

If you have time, you may review your work in this section only.

Page 156

CLOSE YOUR BOOK.

New Jersey Assessment of Skills and Knowledge

LANGUAGE ARTS LITERACY Grade 4

Practice Test 2

Directions to the Student

Read the question on page 159. Write a composition about your favorite season.

You may take notes, create a web, or do other prewriting work in the space provided on pages 160 and 161. Then write your composition on the lines provided on pages 162 and 163.

Here is a checklist for you to follow to help you do your best writing. Please read it silently as I read it aloud to you.

Writer's Checklist

Remember to

❑ Keep the central idea or topic in mind.

❑ Keep your audience in mind.

❑ Support your ideas with details, explanations, and examples.

❑ State your ideas in a clear sequence.

❑ Include an opening and a closing.

❑ Use a variety of words and vary your sentence structure.

❑ State your opinion or conclusion clearly.

❑ Capitalize, spell, and use punctuation correctly.

❑ Write neatly.

After you write your composition, read what you have written.
Use the checklist to make certain that your writing is the best it can be.

Writing Task 1

Most people have a favorite time of year. For some people, it could be summer. Other people might prefer the springtime or fall. What is your favorite time of year?

Write a composition describing your favorite season. Explain why that time of year is so appealing to you.

In your composition, be sure to

- Describe what you tried to do

- Tell why you tried to do it

- Explain how you felt before you tried it

- Explain how you felt after you tried it

- Tell what you learned from your experience.

WRITING TASK 1 – PREWRITING SPACE
Use the space below and on page 161 to plan your writing.

WRITING TASK 1 – PREWRITING SPACE (continued)

Remember — your story must be written on the lines on pages
162 and 163 ONLY.

          TURN TO THE NEXT PAGE.

WRITING TASK 1

My favorite season is Summer.
The thing I like is

WRITING TASK 1 (continued)

_____

_____

_____

_____

_____

_____

_____

_____

_____

_____

_____

_____

_____

_____

_____

_____

If you have time, you may review your work in this section only.

STOP

DO NOT GO ON
UNTIL YOU ARE
TOLD TO DO SO.

Directions to the Student

Now you will read a story and answer the questions that follow.

Some questions will be multiple-choice; others will be open-ended.

1. You may look back at the reading passage as often as you want.

2. Read each question carefully and think about the answer.

3. For each multiple-choice question, select the best answer and fill in the circle next to your choice. Make sure you fill in the correct circle.

4. If you do not know the answer to a question, go on to the next question. You may come back to the skipped question later if you have time.

Rosa's New Job

Rosa looked at the skateboard in the sporting goods store and sighed. "I know," she said to her mother, "we do not have the money for this right now." Mrs. Fernando smiled at Rosa and put her hand around her shoulder.

"Maybe for your birthday," her mother said. Rosa shrugged. Her birthday was more than six months away.

Rosa was tired of not being able to buy the things that she wanted. She was also tired of being the youngest in her family. Her brother and sister both had jobs. They gave a little bit of the money they earned to help the family, but they saved a little for themselves, too. In time, they had enough to buy some of the things they wanted. Rosa wanted to work, too, but what kind of job could a nine-year-old get?

"Carmela and Alberto have jobs," Rosa said. "What kind of job can I do?"

"I have an idea," Mrs. Fernando said, smiling, "but I need to talk to your grandmother before I tell you about it."

That night after dinner, Mrs. Fernando said that she had found a job for Rosa. "You can watch your cousin Pedro after school each day while your grandmother takes a nap," she said. Rosa knew that her grandmother watched Pedro while his mother was at work and that Grandma had looked tired lately.

"That's not really a job," Rosa explained. "Pedro is already three years old, and Grandma will be home to watch me, too. That's too easy. Can't Pedro just play by himself while Grandmother naps?"

Rosa's mother laughed. "Do you want the job or not?" she asked.

Rosa said she would take it.

The next day, Rosa took the bus to her grandmother's apartment building after school. Pedro gave her a high five when she arrived. Rosa picked him up and spun him around. She had planned to spend some time coloring with Pedro while Grandma napped.

Grandma kissed Rosa on the forehead. "Do not let Pedro watch any more television," she said. "Just wake me if you have any problems." Then Grandma headed for her room.

Rosa put the coloring books and crayons on the coffee table in the living room. Pedro turned on the television set and tossed a sofa cushion on the floor.

"No, Pedro," Rosa said. "No television now. Grandma does not want you watching television all day. Now we're going to color."

Pedro turned up the volume on the television. "No, Rosa," he said, and smiled. "Watch TV now!"

Rosa stood and turned off the television set. "Pedro, Grandma said no. You need to sit down and color."

Pedro made a face at Rosa and came over to the table. Pedro drew a line on a piece of paper and broke the crayon. "I do not like coloring, Rosa," he said loudly.

"Okay. If you don't want to color, why don't you let me read you a story?" Rosa picked up one of Pedro's books.

Pedro shook his head, climbed up onto the sofa, and jumped up and down. "Rosa, come play with me!" he shouted.

Rosa pulled him down. "No Pedro, no jumping. Sofas are for sitting, not jumping."

Pedro sat down, but just for a few minutes. Then he took off like lightning for the kitchen and was into the refrigerator. Before Rosa knew what was happening, he broke an egg on the kitchen floor.

While Grandma slept, Pedro ran out into the hallway and kicked and screamed as Rosa dragged him back inside. He spilled his juice on the table and wrapped himself in paper towels. He threw his toys around the living room while singing and dancing.

By the time Grandma woke up from her nap, Rosa was really tired. Grandma asked her to stay for dinner, but Rosa was just too tired.

"So, how was your new job?" Mama asked when Rosa sat down at the dinner table.

"Hard! Pedro is a monster," Rosa replied.

Mama threw her head back and laughed loudly. "No, honey, he's just three, that's all."

Rosa told her mother about how she spent most of the afternoon chasing after Pedro. "He doesn't listen to me," she said. "I don't think I can do my job. He will not be quiet, and he made a huge mess." Rosa put some salad on her plate and tried to hold back the tears.

"What did you ask Pedro to do with you?" Mama asked.

"I wanted him to color, and then I tried to read him a story, but instead I wound up chasing him around and trying to keep him from breaking things."

"Pedro likes to move around and has trouble sitting still," Mama concluded. "Maybe tomorrow you need to do something more active with him."

Rosa smiled. She had an idea.

The next day she arrived at Grandma's with some CDs in her book bag. Just like yesterday, when Pedro saw her he gave her a high five. And then, just like yesterday, he tossed a sofa cushion onto the floor and turned on the television.

Rosa calmly turned it off. "Let's do something better," she said. "Watching television is boring. How about I teach you to dance?"

Pedro jumped up and clapped his hands, and Rosa put on a CD. Rosa started to dance and Pedro did what she did. Then Pedro danced and Rosa did what he did. When they couldn't dance any more, they marched around the house like soldiers. Then they played hide-and-seek. Rosa was once again exhausted when Grandma woke up from her nap, but she felt as if she had done a much better job with Pedro.

"Rosa, are you coming over tomorrow?" Pedro asked as Rosa was leaving.

"You bet," she said, happy to have discovered that saving money to buy a skateboard could be so fun.

1. **At the beginning of the story, why does Rosa sigh while gazing at the skateboard?**

    Ⓐ She knows that her mother cannot buy it for her.

    Ⓑ She does not think it would be a good birthday gift.

    Ⓒ She thinks that Pedro would probably damage it.

    Ⓓ She knows it will be hard to find a job to help pay for it.

2. **How is Rosa's first day of watching Pedro different from how she thought it would be?**

    Ⓐ She thought it would be hard work, but it was a lot of fun.

    Ⓑ She thought it would be noisy, but it was very quiet.

    Ⓒ She thought it would be exciting, but it was very dull.

    Ⓓ She thought it would be easy, but it was very difficult.

3. **How does Rosa's mother help Rosa prepare for the next time she watches Pedro?**

    Ⓐ She tells Rosa to teach Pedro how to do different dances.

    Ⓑ She suggests that Rosa get help with Pedro from her grandmother.

    Ⓒ She tells Rosa to make Pedro do things that use more energy.

    Ⓓ She suggests that Rosa let Pedro do whatever he wants to do.

4. What is a theme of "Rosa's New Job"?

Ⓐ You should give up when things don't go your way.

Ⓑ It's good to work hard for the things you want.

Ⓒ It's difficult to try to care for young children.

● Family is the most important thing in life.

5. In the passage, Rosa notices that her grandmother has been looking tired. Why does she look so tired?

Ⓐ She has not been feeling well lately.

Ⓑ She is no longer able to sleep at night.

Ⓒ She works at several different jobs.

● She has been busy chasing after Pedro.

6. What does the phrase "took off like lightning" from the sentence "Then he took off like lightning for the kitchen and was into the refrigerator" tell you about Pedro?

Ⓐ He is always hungry.

Ⓑ He is afraid of big storms.

Ⓒ He likes Rosa's cooking.

● He gets into trouble quickly.

TURN TO THE NEXT PAGE. ➡

7. **What does the word "active" mean in the sentence "Maybe tomorrow you need to do something more active with him"?**

    Ⓐ calming and quiet

    Ⓑ with a lot of movement

    Ⓒ away from other people

    Ⓓ involving the imagination

8. **At the end of the story when Rosa says "you bet," she means that**

    Ⓐ she has enough money to buy her skateboard.

    Ⓑ she wants Pedro to guess whether or not she will come back.

    Ⓒ of course she will come back to play with Pedro.

    Ⓓ next time she wants Pedro to go to her house to play.

9. **How does Pedro change by the end of the story?**

    Ⓐ He no longer wants to just watch TV.

    Ⓑ He is happy to go to Rosa's house.

    Ⓒ He learns to sit still and read books.

    Ⓓ He no longer wants Grandma to watch him.

> # For the open-ended questions on the next page, remember to
>
> - Focus your response on the question asked.
> - Answer all parts of the question.
> - Give a complete explanation.
> - Use specific information from the story.

She wants the money

Rosa

She doesn't care about the job she lost

wants the skateboard

10. When Rosa sees the skateboard in the store, she decides that she wants to get a job in order to make some money to buy the things she wants. Explain what this shows about Rosa.

Use information from the story to support your response.

Write your answer on the lines below.

_____

_____

_____

_____

_____

_____

_____

_____

_____

_____

_____

_____

_____

_____

If you have time, you may review your work in this section only.

Directions to the Student

Read the poem "The Hayloft" to yourself while I read it aloud to you. Afterward, you will do a writing task. The poem may give you ideas for your writing.

The Hayloft

by Robert Louis Stevenson

Through all the pleasant meadow-side
The grass grew shoulder-high,
Till the shining scythes went far and wide
And cut it down to dry.

Those green and sweetly smelling crops
They led in waggons home;
And they piled them here in mountain tops
For mountaineers to roam.

Here is Mount Clear, Mount Rusty-Nail,
Mount Eagle and Mount High;—
The mice that in these mountains dwell,
No happier are than I!

Oh, what a joy to clamber there,
Oh, what a place for play,
With the sweet, the dim, the dusty air,
The happy hills of hay!

Writing Task 2

In "The Hayloft," the poet Robert Louis Stevenson writes about a child's favorite place to play. Most of us have a favorite place where we like to go to play, think, or relax. Write a composition about your favorite place.

In your composition, be sure to

- **Describe where your favorite place is and what you do there.**

- **Give details about how this place looks, feels, sounds, and smells.**

- **Explain why you like to go there so much.**

You may take notes, create a web, or do other prewriting work in the space provided on pages 175 and 176. Then, write your composition on the lines provided on pages 177 and 178.

Here is a checklist for you to follow to help you do your best writing. Please read it silently as I read it aloud to you.

Writer's Checklist

Remember to

❑ Keep the central idea or topic in mind.

❑ Keep your audience in mind.

❑ Support your ideas with details, explanations, and examples.

❑ State your ideas in a clear sequence.

❑ Include an opening and a closing.

❑ Use a variety of words and vary your sentence structure.

❑ State your opinion or conclusion clearly.

❑ Capitalize, spell, and use punctuation correctly.

❑ Write neatly.

After you write your composition, read what you have written. Use the checklist to make certain that your writing is the best it can be.

WRITING TASK 2 – PREWRITING SPACE

Use the space below and on page 176 to plan your writing.

3

WRITING TASK 2 – PREWRITING SPACE (continued)

Remember — your composition must be written on the lines on
pages 177 and 178 ONLY.

WRITING TASK 2

My favorite place to realax play and think is in my back yard. The thing I do there is play soccer chill, and some times do my H.W. This place looks fun, feels happy, and smells fresh. The reason I like to go their so much is because the weather is getting nicer and nicer.

WRITING TASK 2 (continued)

If you have time, you may review your work in this section only.

STOP

DO NOT GO ON UNTIL YOU ARE TOLD TO DO SO.

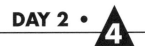

Directions to the Student

In the following section, you will read a passage and answer the questions that follow.

Some questions will be multiple-choice; others will be open-ended.

1. You may look back at the reading passage as often as you want.

2. Read each question carefully and think about the answer.

3. For each multiple-choice question, select the best answer and fill in the circle next to your choice. Make sure you fill in the correct circle.

4. If you do not know the answer to a question, go on to the next question. You may come back to the skipped question later if you have time.

TURN TO THE NEXT PAGE. ➡

Directions: Read the story and answer the questions that follow.

The Great Car and Dog Wash

"It's a great idea," Maddie's big brother Ryan said to his friend Jackson. Maddie was listening outside the door of her brother's room. She did not want to risk being seen and told to "scram," but she was interested in what they were talking about. Ryan was in ninth grade and Maddie was in fourth. She sighed. It sure was tough being a little sister.

"The Haddonfield Nature Preserve is such a great place," Jackson was saying. "It would be terrible if the town turned it into a golf course."

"Right." Ryan said. "But the town cannot afford to take care of the preserve. A golf course would bring them more money."

"So, we'll raise the money to save the preserve!" Jackson said.

"A car wash is a start," Ryan agreed, "but we'll have to do more."

At that, Maddie went back into her own room to think. The Haddonfield Nature Preserve was one of her favorite places. Her family went on walks there almost every weekend, and her summer day camp met there every year. What would happen if they turned it into a golf course? It sure would be terrible! Maddie wanted to help protect the preserve, too.

That night at dinner she said, "So, Ryan, are the ninth graders having a car wash or something? I heard some kids talking about it…"

Ryan looked sternly at Maddie. This was not the first time she listened in to his private conversations. "Yeah, who wants to know?"

"Ryan, if the Haddonfield Nature Preserve needs money, then I want to help, too!"

"Car washes are not for little kids, Maddie," Ryan said in a nicer tone. "It is great that you want to help, but a car wash is lots of work."

Maddie was discouraged. She called her friend Janine after dinner to talk about it.

"It's true that washing cars might be hard," Janine said. "But maybe we can help by washing something smaller." Janine was always good for an idea.

"Yes!" Maddie said, excited. "People need to wash their dogs, right? Especially in the spring when it is so muddy out. Why don't we set up a dog washing station at the car wash? That way people can bring their dogs in their cars and get them both washed!"

"You know, I think that might work!" Janine shrieked in a high-pitched voice.

So Maddie and Janine talked to their teachers who said that they would talk to the grade nine teachers. Everyone thought that the dog wash was a great way for Maddie and her friends to help raise money for the preserve.

The day of the great Haddonfield Car and Dog Wash was a great success! Everyone in town with a dog drove over to the high school parking lot to watch their cars and their dogs get scrubbed clean. People without dogs came with their cars and had a great time watching the scene while their cars were polished to shining.

Maddie and Janine were as proud as peacocks with how much money they raised for the Haddonfield Nature Preserve. Even Ryan smiled at Maddie and said, "Great job, sis." And what more could a little sister ask for?

11. **Why does Maddie most likely think it is difficult to be a little sister?**

   Ⓐ Her brother never wants to play with her.

   Ⓑ She is never allowed to do anything difficult.

   Ⓒ She always has to go to summer day camp.

   Ⓓ Her teachers always compare her to her brother.

12. **What is a theme of "The Great Car and Dog Wash"?**

   Ⓐ If you fail at first, try again and you will succeed.

   Ⓑ Helping people is the most important part of life.

   Ⓒ Even kids can do something to help a cause.

   Ⓓ Be true to your friends, no matter what.

13. **What might have happened in the story if Maddie had not called Janine after dinner?**

   Ⓐ Janine might have decided to try to ruin Ryan's car wash.

   Ⓑ Maddie might have forgotten about Ryan and Jackson's plan.

   Ⓒ The car and dog wash might not have been a success.

   Ⓓ The girls might not have thought of doing a dog wash.

14. **Which of these best describes how Ryan probably feels about Maddie?**

    Ⓐ He wishes that he did not have a sister.

    Ⓑ He thinks that she is the funniest person he knows.

    Ⓒ He likes her, but sometimes finds her annoying.

    Ⓓ He wants her to spend more time with him and his friends.

15. **What does the word "sternly" mean in the sentence "Ryan looked sternly at Maddie"?**

    Ⓐ angrily

    Ⓑ happily

    Ⓒ sadly

    Ⓓ wearily

16. **What does it tell you about Janine that she "shrieked in a high-pitched voice"?**

    Ⓐ She has a beautiful singing voice.

    Ⓑ She often bothers people with her loud voice.

    Ⓒ She is excited about doing a car and dog wash.

    Ⓓ She is easily frightened by very large dogs.

     TURN TO THE NEXT PAGE. ▶

17. **What do you think will happen now that the dog and car wash is over?**

    Ⓐ Maddie and Ryan will split the money from the car and dog wash.

    ● The students will think of more ways to raise money for the preserve.

    © The Haddonfield Nature Preserve will be shut down until the summer.

    Ⓓ Janine and Jackson will take all the credit for the car and dog wash.

18. **Why is it so important for the story to take place in the spring?**

    Ⓐ Maddie and Janine were not friends in the fall.

    Ⓑ People do not drive their cars in the winter.

    © The children are too busy with camp in the summer.

    ● Dogs are often very dirty in the spring.

19. **Which phrase from the story best describes how Maddie and Janine feel about their success?**

    ● proud as peacocks

    Ⓑ polished to shining

    © had a great time

    Ⓓ that might work

For the open-ended question on the next page, remember to

- Focus your response on the question asked.

- Answer all parts of the question.

- Give a complete explanation.

- Use specific information from the story.

TURN TO THE NEXT PAGE.

20. Whose idea was better, Ryan's or Janine's? Why do you think so?
     Use information from the story to support your response.

     Write your answer on the lines below.

_____

_____

_____

_____

_____

_____

_____

_____

_____

_____

_____

_____

_____

If you have time, you may review your work in this section only.

**DO NOT GO ON
UNTIL YOU ARE
TOLD TO DO SO.**

Directions: Read the article and answer the questions that follow.

A Beginner's Guide to Hamster Care

If you are thinking of getting a family pet, there are a number of things to keep in mind. Remember that any pet needs a lot of time and attention in order to be happy and healthy. Make sure you have enough time in your daily life to take care of and play with a pet. When you are ready, then you can decide what pet is best for you. Each kind of pet has different needs. You need to have a lot of space to keep a horse. You need to have time to walk a dog several times a day. Perhaps you might consider a hamster. Furry hamsters make wonderful friends and are easy to care for. Why not learn more about hamsters and add them to your list of possible pets for your family?

What do I need to know about hamsters?

Hamsters are part of the rodent family, along with mice and rats. There are two kinds of hamsters that people most commonly keep as pets, Syrian hamsters and Dwarf hamsters.

Syrian hamsters are slightly bigger than other kinds of hamsters. They need to be housed in their own cages; they do not like being housed in groups and will fight with other hamsters. Consider a Syrian if you only want to keep one hamster in a cage.

Dwarf hamsters are smaller than Syrian hamsters. They actually prefer the company of other Dwarf hamsters, so it is all right to have more than one in a cage. Consider Dwarf hamsters if you want to keep several together.

Both Syrian and Dwarf hamsters come in a number of different colors, ranging from tan to black, and some hamsters are even snow white in color.

TURN TO THE NEXT PAGE.

Which hamster should I choose?

It is very important that you take a careful look at the pet store where you buy your hamster. Make sure that the pet store is clean and that the pets seem happy and healthy. When you find a pet store that you like, pick the right kind and color of hamster for you. You might want to go to the pet store in the late afternoon, when the hamsters will more likely be awake and playing in their cages. This way, you will get to see what each hamster is like, whether it is lively or shy. Seeing a hamster at play helps you to decide which hamster suits you the best.

What does a hamster need?

You will need to buy several things along with your hamster. First, you will need a suitable cage. Because Syrian hamsters are larger, they need larger cages than Dwarf hamsters need. Simple metal cages can work for Syrian hamsters, but the spaces between the bars might be too large for the smaller hamsters. Glass or plastic cages are better for smaller hamsters. All hamsters like to have room to move around, so make sure that the cage you buy has plenty of space in which your hamster can play.

Along with the cage, you will also need to buy bedding and nesting material. This is usually made up of pine wood shavings and thin strips of paper. Do not buy cotton or plastic bedding as it might hurt your hamster. You will need to change the bedding in the cage at least once a week, so make sure that you buy enough.

Hamsters love to play, just as people do. You can buy small balls for hamsters to chase around the cage or long tubes for them to run through. And no hamster cage is complete without a hamster wheel, where your new pet can run to keep in shape.

What do hamsters eat?

Most hamsters like leafy green vegetables, such lettuce and spinach, best. They will also eat cooked chicken or beef and cheese, as well as cooked eggs and cereals with little or no sugar. It is important that your hamster drink plenty of clean water. Be sure that you change your hamster's water every day.

How do I keep my hamster happy and healthy?

Life with a hamster can be rewarding, as long as you treat your hamster well. All hamsters, no matter what type, sleep during the day and are active during the evening hours. This means that hamsters will most likely not want to play during the day. Make sure that you have time after school or at night to give your hamster some attention. Feel free to take your hamster out of the cage to play if the hamster seems interested. Always be very gentle when handling your hamster, and keep any other animals out of the room while you play. You can roll a ball around for your hamster or let it explore the room a bit. Just be sure that your hamster cannot become lost in your house while it is outside of its cage.

Enjoy getting to know your hamster and have fun!

21. **What is the purpose of the first paragraph?**

Ⓐ to help readers understand how to get ready to choose a pet

Ⓑ to tell readers what to do when caring for dogs

Ⓒ to explain to readers why horses need lots of room

Ⓓ to give readers a list of animals that make wonderful pets

22. **Why is it important to keep Syrian hamsters away from other hamsters?**

Ⓐ Syrian hamsters are afraid of other hamsters.

Ⓑ Syrian hamsters are much smaller than other hamsters.

Ⓒ Syrian hamsters will fight other hamsters.

Ⓓ The food Syrian hamsters eat is different from the food other hamsters eat.

23. **Why might a glass or plastic cage be better for a smaller hamster?**

Ⓐ The hamster would have more room to run around.

Ⓑ The hamster could have more toys to play with.

Ⓒ The plastic and glass cages let in more light.

Ⓓ The plastic and glass cages are more secure.

24.　Why should you shop for a hamster in the afternoon or evening?

   Ⓐ　Hamsters are often eating their dinners during the afternoon or evening.

   Ⓑ　Hamsters are more likely to be awake during the afternoon or evening.

   Ⓒ　There will be fewer people in the pet store during the afternoon or evening.

   Ⓓ　There are more people at the pet store to help you during the afternoon or evening.

25.　What does the word "company" mean in the sentence "They actually prefer the company of other Dwarf hamsters, so it is all right to have more than one in a cage"?

   Ⓐ　a local pet store

   Ⓑ　a group of performers

   Ⓒ　the closeness of friends

   Ⓓ　the fun of having a pet

26.　Why did the author MOST LIKELY write this passage?

   Ⓐ　to encourage people to adopt a pet

   Ⓑ　to tell readers where to buy a hamster

   Ⓒ　to show readers the different pets to adopt

   Ⓓ　to explain how to care for a pet hamster

27. If you did not spend enough time with your hamster, it would probably

Ⓐ feel sad and might get sick.

Ⓑ fight with the other hamsters.

Ⓒ escape from its cage and run away.

Ⓓ be eaten by other pets in the house.

28. Why does the author use questions for all the section headings?

Ⓐ to help the reader locate information about pet hamsters

Ⓑ to encourage the reader to think of other pet questions

Ⓒ to persuade the reader get another kind of pet

Ⓓ to show that article was written by a hamster expert

29. In which section of the article can you find information about what to put in your hamster's cage?

Ⓐ What do I need to know about hamsters?

Ⓑ Which hamster should I choose?

Ⓒ What does a hamster need?

Ⓓ How do I keep my hamster happy and healthy?

For the open-ended question on the next page, remember to

- Focus your response on the question asked.
- Answer all parts of the question.
- Give a complete explanation.
- Use specific information from the article.

TURN TO THE NEXT PAGE.

5

30. After reading this article, do you think that a hamster would be a good pet for you? Why or why not? Use details from the article in your answer.

Write your answer on the lines below.

_____

_____

_____

_____

_____

_____

_____

_____

_____

_____

_____

_____

_____

_____

_____

_____

If you have time, you may review your work in this section only.

STOP

CLOSE YOUR BOOK.

Answer Key

Chapter 1 Answer Explanations

W1   Recognizing a Central Idea or Theme
W2   Recognizing Supporting Details

Passage 1: "Tanya's Wish"

1. **B**

   If you reread the third paragraph, you will see that Tanya likes to wish on planes when she sees them go by.

2. **C**

   Tanya's mother is trying to give Tanya a dish towel. Her mother says that Tanya is supposed to be helping her in the kitchen.

3. **D**

   If you reread this story, you will see that Tanya waits patiently for a chance to go on a plane. By the end of the story, she gets her reward. She gets to take a plane trip.

Passage 2: "Changing the Sound of Music"

1. **B**

   When you read this selection, you can see Count Basie played in a band that broke up in Kansas City. Then Count Basie joined another band that traveled a little.

2. **D**

   An announcer told William Basie that the name "Count" made him sound like a better band leader.

3. **A**

   This story tells about the life and music of Count Basie. The title offers a clue.

Passage 3: "Annie and the School Shopper"

1. **C**

   Susan is in better shape in school because she is prepared. The theme is that hard work is best or that you should be prepared.

2. **C**

   Susan's bags were filled with pens, pencils, notebooks, paper, a dictionary, and a thesaurus. (W2)

3. **C**

   Annie lies on the towel in the sun by the pool while Susan gets ready for school. (W2)

4. **B**

   Most of the first paragraph is about why Annie prefers summer to being in school. (W1)

Chapter 2 Answer Explanations

W4   Paraphrasing/Retelling (Vocabulary)
A2   Predicting Tentative Meanings

New Words

The word "sluggish" means "slow."

The context clues include that Christina's eyes were only opened halfway and she wanted to return to bed.

Words with More Than One Meaning

In the first sentence, "light" means "a lamp." In the second sentence, "light" means "does not weigh much."

In the first sentence, "foil" means "a covering." In the second sentence it means "stopped."

Passage 1: "Max Has a Dream"

1. C

The word "deserted" means empty. Max thinks that there is no one on the island. (A2)

2. B

The word "cautious" means careful. Max takes his time as he looks around. (W4)

Passage 2: "Farming Forever"

1. C

The word "appreciate" means to "be glad about." The author thinks that if you go on a hayride through the pumpkin patch at Shamrock Farms, you will be glad about autumn.

2. D

When the butter separates from the cream, it moves away from it. Then the cream is removed and put into a bowl.

3. B

In this article, the word "pinch" means "a little bit." The author says she sprinkles in just a pinch or two of salt for flavor.

Passage 3: Excerpt from *The Wonderful Wizard of Oz*

1. C

When the Tin Woodman stands motionless, he does not move. If you did not know the answer to this question, the words "as if he could not stir at all" offer a clue that he is not moving.

2. D

The word "comrade" means "friend." The Tin Woodman is their new friend.

3. A

The only answer choice that makes sense is answer choice A: deeply. Dorothy is so lost in her thoughts that she doesn't even notice when Scarecrow falls.

4. A

The word "inquired" means "asked." The question mark at the end of the sentence offers a clue.

Chapter 3 Answer Explanations

W3   Extrapolating Information and Following Directions

W5   Recognizing Text Organization

Passage 1: "Any Way the Wind Blows"

1. **B**

   The first paragraph is used to explain to the reader what wind vanes are used for. The author explains how wind vanes are used to tell us what direction the wind is coming from and how the information is helpful in many different ways.

2. **A**

   Step 9 tells the reader to ask the adult to adjust the pin if the straw doesn't spin smoothly around the tip of the pencil.

3. Answers will vary.

   Sample answer: The purpose of the last paragraph is to show the reader how to use the wind vane. The author tells the readers that they must find all of the directions first before they can use the wind vane. After they know where each direction is, they can use the wind vane to see which way the wind is blowing.

Passage 2: "Play Time"

1. **B**

   The words in dark print are the most important tips given in the passage. They divide the passage into different sections, each describing a step in preparing for a play.

2. **B**

   In this section of the article, the author explains that accidents happen and things go wrong when people perform. She says to have a good time because she does not want you to be anxious about performing. She wants you to stay calm and relaxed.

3. Answers will vary.

   Sample answer: In the article, it says that an understudy takes the place of an actor or an actress who gets sick. It's a good idea to have understudies, because then if an actor or an actress gets sick, you can still go on with the play. Without understudies, you might have to wait until the actor or actress gets better to perform the play.

Passage 3: "Inventing Ideas"

1. **C**

   The author adds a note to this passage, right under the materials list, to add information the reader needs. Since the newspapers and magazines will be cut up during the exercise, the reader should be sure nobody else needs them!

2. **B**

   In Exercise 1, it says that you can make a story out of a picture, such as a painting, just by looking at it and asking yourself questions. Your questions (and answers) may begin helping you to think of a new story.

3. Answers will vary.

   Sample answer: This passage gives two exercises to help people think of new story ideas. The first exercise is all about looking at pictures. By finding an interesting picture, thinking about it, and asking yourself questions about it, you can find some great ideas. The second exercise talks about filling up hats with newspaper headlines and magazine pictures. By choosing headlines and pictures, you can come up with many different ideas. If I needed a new idea, I would try the second exercise. It seems like more fun, and I would like to use words and pictures together. On top of that, it would also be fun to cut up a lot of old magazines!

Chapter 4 Answer Explanations

W6   Recognizing a Purpose for Reading
W5   Recognizing Text Organization
A2   Predicting Tentative Meanings

Author's Purpose

1. convince
2. teach or instruct
3. entertain
4. inform or describe
5. describe
6. inform

Prediction

Answers will vary.

Sample answer: Angela will remember the rule about which comes first, "i" or "e," right before she spells the word. She has studied very hard and she knows how to spell the word. She just needs to remember it.

Some students might argue that Angela will not remember the word. They might think that she is too confused to spell the word correctly.

Passage 1: "The Wonders of Breakfast"

1. **C**

    By looking at the entire passage, the reader can tell that the author wants readers to eat a healthy breakfast every day. The author tells the readers why breakfast is important and then gives the readers a recipe for an omelet to try.

2. **B**

    After reading the passage, the reader should be able to tell that the author does not think it is okay to skip breakfast at any time. The reader can also see that the author does not think that sugary foods like doughnuts should be eaten at breakfast.

3. **D**

    In this sentence, the author is not suggesting that vegetables don't taste good in the morning or that someone told her not to eat vegetables in the morning. The author also doesn't say anything about most people not liking vegetables. He is suggesting that many people don't eat vegetables in the morning.

4. **C**

    The recipe tells you how to make an omelet.

Passage 2: "New Jersey's Pine Barrens"

1. **C**

    The second paragraph tells readers that the Pine Barrens is in southern New Jersey and that roads pass through it to connect major cities.

2. **A**

    In this passage, the author tells the history of the Pine Barrens. He or she identifies what the Pine Barrens is and then explains its history from the time of the Native Americans to the present day.

3. **B**

    Judging by the author's ideas, he or she would probably agree that forests can be useful and beautiful. In the passage, he or she explains that the Pine Barrens was originally known for its beauty, but also that it has provided people with food, wood, and other resources.

Passage 4: Excerpt from *Rebecca of Sunnybrook Farm*

1. **B**

    The purpose of this story is to entertain. It tells the story of a little girl going on a trip.

2. **A**

    While the second paragraph tells about a woman in the coach, its purpose is to show that you Mr. Cobb didn't consider it his job to make passengers comfortable.

3. Answers will vary.

    Sample answer: I think Rebecca will get into some trouble or will perhaps talk to the woman in the coach and get to know her. The fact that Rebecca yells out the window that she had taken her nightgown on the last trip, even though her mother tells her not to talk like this, shows that she is very outgoing and a little bit bold.

Chapter 5 Answer Explanations

A1 Questioning, Clarifying, Predicting
A3 Forming Opinions about Text and Author's Techniques
A4 Making Judgments, Drawing Conclusions

Passage 1: "A Giant Discovery"

1. A

You can conclude from the last paragraph of the passage that the small stone marks the place where the dinosaur skeleton was found, so that people will remember this special place. You can also find this answer by using the process of elimination. We don't know for sure that other dinosaur bones might be there (answer choice A). In fact, there probably are not, or they would have already been discovered. And looking at the small stone probably won't make people want to travel to Philadelphia to see the dinosaur skeleton (answer choice C). And we can't conclude that the purpose of the stone is to tell people where to go to see the dinosaur (answer choice D). Answer choice A is the best answer.

2. D

The passage says that the mayor gave the dinosaur the key to the city and named the dinosaur an honorary citizen. This shows that he must have been very excited about the discovery.

3. Answers will vary.

Sample answer: This is the first complete dinosaur skeleton, and scientists learned a great deal from it. They learned that dinosaurs really existed and that they walked on two legs.

Passage 2: "The Cape May Lighthouse"

1. C

The third lighthouse was built six hundred feet away from the second lighthouse. This is far away, and the second lighthouse washed away. Therefore, the third lighthouse was probably built in a safer place.

2. A

The lighthouse is lit by electricity today, so there is probably no longer a need for a keeper to live by the lighthouse.

3. C

Few people are on the beach during the winter, because it is very cold. This is the most likely reason that the lighthouse is not open to the public during this time.

4. Answers will vary.

Sample answer: I think it would be great fun to visit the Cape May Lighthouse. I would like to try to climb all of those stairs, and I would really like to see the entire Cape May peninsula.

Passage 3: "Maria Tallchief"

1. C

Maria's dance teacher in California said she had to relearn everything that she had learned and that she wasn't yet ready to wear pointe shoes. You can tell from this that her dance teachers in Oklahoma did not know as much about ballet as they should have.

2. Answers will vary.

Sample answer: I think Maria would make a great teacher. She obviously knows a great deal about ballet, and at the end of the article, she says that she wants to encourage dancers to make the dance steps their own. This sounds like great advice to me.

3. Answers will vary.

Sample answer: Maria's mother helped her by encouraging her to learn all she could about music. Her family had her begin taking piano lessons when she was only four. When she later took dance lessons and became very good at dancing, they moved to California, where there were better dance teachers. This must have been a difficult thing to do. They probably sacrificed a great deal, but it did help Maria greatly. I think this is the way in which they helped her the most.

Chapter 6 Answer Explanations

A5   Interpreting Literary Elements and Textual Conventions
W5   Recognizing Text Organization

Characters

The two characters in "A Helping Hand" are Paul and David.

Special Language and Type

1. The author put the words in italics to show that these are words that Beth is writing in her journal.

2. Beth calls her journal her "dear old friend" because she writes all of her feelings down in it and she feels that the journal is like an old friend who knows her very well.

Passage 1: Excerpt from *O Pioneers!*

1. **B**

   Carl is the main character. The story introduces him as the first character and follows him through the passage.

2. **C**

   The first few lines of the story tell the reader that the story takes place on a day in July. July is in the summer.

3. **B**

   Carl's friends come over because they are on their way to buy a hammock. They ask him to join them and he gets on their wagon. The wagon is the place where most of the story takes place.

Passage 2: Excerpt from *The Selfish Giant*

1. **D**

   The title of the story actually tells you who the main character in this story is. The story is mostly about the Selfish Giant and what he does. The other characters are not the main focus of the story.

2. **C**

   The words in capital letters are on the sign. This sign warns readers to stay away. The author does this to show the reader the sign's function.

3. **D**

   Because Snow and Frost are elements of the weather and not real people, the fact that they can talk in this story tells the reader that this story is make-believe. All of the other things are events that could take place in real life.

Passage 3: "Making a Big Sound"

1. **B**

   The story is about Jason. Jason is the character who says and does the most.

2. **C**

   Jason wanted to play an instrument that he thought was important to the band. When he is given the tambourine, he thinks that it is an instrument that doesn't really matter. He doesn't believe that the tambourine is an important instrument.

3. **A**

   The words in italics are Jason's thoughts. You can tell that they are his thoughts because the word "I" is used. You can also tell that they are his thoughts because they are followed by the words "thought Jason."

4. Answers will vary.

   Sample answer: Ms. Chase helps Jason to understand that all of the instruments are important by having the band play the song once without the tambourine. When she asks Jason to join the band, he listens to how the tambourine changes the song. The tambourine makes the song better, and this helps Jason to see that all of the instruments in a song matter.

Practice Test 1 Answer Explanations

Writing Task 1

Sample answer:

The last time I went to visit my cousins in Paramus, I played chess for the first time. Chess always seemed too hard for me, so I was sort of scared to learn. But my cousins Rita and Will play all the time, and I did not want to feel left out. Rita and Will taught me all the rules. It was complicated! Each piece moves in a different way. I thought I would never remember it all. But my cousins were good teachers.

After they explained the rules, we played a practice game. As we played, they coached me on how to move my pieces. Gradually I learned how to move the knights, pawns, rooks, bishops, king, and queen. The queen was my favorite because you can move her any way you want. But my cousins explained to me how I should protect my queen until I really needed her. Finally, I played a game against Rita without any coaching, and I did great! Well, I did not win, but I remembered all the rules.

Before I played chess, I though the game was such a mystery. Mysteries can be scary. But after I learned to play, chess was not such a mystery. It is still a challenge, though, but a challenge I can now face without fear. The most important thing I learned from the experience is that if you learn more about something you are scared of, it is not so scary anymore.

"One More Chance..."

1. **D** A5 Literary Elements and Textual Conventions

    The purpose of the flashback is to show that Ryan never improved as a baseball player, from the first practice to the end of the season.

2. **C** W1 Central Idea

    Ryan has been a bad baseball player since the first practice. He has a dream that he costs his team the chance to be in the playoffs. Even so, Ryan still looks in the mirror and whispers, "One more chance," proving that he still believes that he will one day get better at baseball.

3. **B** W4 Paraphrasing/Vocabulary

    The word "walloped" means "struck" or "hit." Answer choice B is correct.

4.   **C**   W2   Supporting Details

After Ryan strikes out, he probably feels troubled. He really wanted to help his team make it to the playoffs, but he failed to help them win.

5.   **D**   A5   Literary Elements and Textual Conventions

The expression "his face as blank as an empty desktop" is a simile that the author uses to compare the Giants' pitcher's face to and empty desktop. This comparison shows that the pitcher was standing on the mound with no expression on his face. We know from the story that this is an important point in the game, so the pitcher must be thinking very hard, or concentrating, on what he is doing.

6.   **B**   A4   Making Judgments, Drawing Conclusions

Earlier in the story, Ryan says that his teammates cross their fingers when he is at bat, hoping that he gets a hit. They want him to hit the ball, and if he did, they would be surprised, but they would certainly cheer happily.

7.   **B**   A5   Literary Elements and Textual Conventions

The only words in the story that are in italics are Ryan's thoughts. The author shares Ryan's thoughts in this way to give the reader a more direct understanding of Ryan's personality and feelings.

8.   **A**   W3   Extrapolation of Information

At the end of the story, Ryan is confused because he has been dreaming about the final baseball game before the playoffs. He thinks he has already let his team down, when really the game has not yet taken place.

9.   **A**   W6   Recognition of a Purpose for Reading

This story is inspiring in that when Ryan wakes up from his dream, he does not feel discouraged by what happened. Instead, he is inspired to try harder in the game, despite his tough season.

10.   Answers will vary.   A1   Questioning/Clarifying/Predicting,
A3   Forming of Opinions

Sample answer: During the story, we learn that Ryan is not a very good baseball player. He has never hit the ball in all his turns at bat. The fact that Ryan is even still on the team shows that he is not a person who likes to give up. It must have been difficult to play the entire season knowing that his teammates were hoping so hard for him to get a hit. The fact that Ryan is so happy to have "one more chance" at the end of the story says several things about him. He is probably a really nice guy and a good friend to his

teammates. If he was not, his teammates probably would not really want him on the team. Ryan also seems to have an extremely positive attitude. He did not have a great season, then he had a terrible dream about losing an important game for the team. Still, he woke up excited to get out there and play the game. That sort of positive attitude is important to have in life—it is better to look forward than to look backward.

"To Sleep, Perhaps to Dream"

11. **C   W4   Paraphrasing, Vocabulary**

The word "recover" means "get back to the original state" or "get back to normal." We all need to recover from a busy day by resting and sleeping, just as we need to recover from a cold by taking it easy and drinking plenty of water.

12. **D   W2   Recognition of Supporting Details**

In the section "To process information" the author writes about how dreams, even strange ones, help us process information and preserve memories.

13. **A   A4   Making Judgments, Drawing Conclusions**

Most people know from experience that after a day full of physical activity, it is easier to fall asleep and to sleep deeply. The author also states this in the "To recover from activity" section of the article.

14. **A   A2   Prediction of Tentative Meaning**

The word "funny" can have several different meanings. The reader knows from the context and probably from their own lives that some dreams can make them feel strange.

15. **D   W5   Recognition of Text Organization**

The author states that the light from the TV screen tricks the brain into staying active and makes it harder for you to go to sleep.

16. **D   A5   Literary Elements and Textual Conventions**

The exclamation at the beginning of the article creates a connection between the reader and all the other people around the world who hear a similar wake-up call. It shows that sleep is universal and personal at the same time.

17. C W1 Recognition of a Central Idea or Theme

The other answer choices involve specific details from the article. The article is more generally about the sleep habits of people and animals.

18. D A2 Prediction of Tentative Meaning

The author does not state specifically why dolphins sleep with only one side of their brains at a time. The reader needs to make an assumption based on information from the article and outside knowledge. Dolphins are probably prey to sharks and other fish, so they need to keep half awake to sense when dangerous fish are approaching.

19. B A4 Making Judgments, Drawing Conclusions

The television, computer screen, and light in general are all things that make sleeping more difficult. It is best to sleep away from these things in a comfortable bed, under warm covers, and perhaps with the window open for fresh air.

20. Answers will vary. A1/A4 Questioning, Clarifying, Predicting/ Making Judgments, Drawing Conclusions

Sample answer: If I had trouble sleeping one night and only slept for five hours, I would have a hard time doing much of anything the next day. Five hours is only about half the sleep I need in a night. After a night like that, I would have a difficult time concentrating in school and on my homework. My body would probably be too tired to do sports or maybe even to walk home from school. I might get sick because my immune system would not be very strong. Getting too little sleep is not good for anyone, especially a growing fourth grader like me!

Writing Task 2

Sample answer: Once, I had a dream that I was in a town made of sweets. Everyone in the town was very nice to me and wanted me to try all different kinds of candy, cookies, and cakes. The town had streets of ribbon candy, fountains of soda and syrup, and clouds made of pink and blue cotton candy. The houses and businesses were all made of gingerbread and icing. And the whole town smelled like vanilla icing. I think that if this town were a real place, I would visit it. I think it would be fun, like being in a real-life version of the game Candy Land. Of course, I wouldn't stay too long, for fear that I might get a bellyache.

"Local Girl on a Mission to Save the Planet"

21. A   W5   Text Organization

The first paragraph does not explain ways to save water in your home (B), ways Amanda Carlisle once wasted water (C), or why you should pick up litter (D). The correct answer is A.

22. C   W4   Paraphrasing/Vocabulary

In this sentence, the word "conserve" means "save." When you practice "conservation," it means that you try not to waste too much. You try to conserve, or save, what you use.

23. B   A4   Making Judgments, Drawing Conclusions

According to the article, Amanda was "on her father's case" to fix the dripping faucet. This means that she kept asking him to do it. She was upset about the faucet because it was causing so much water to be wasted. Amanda is good at persuading her family members to conserve water and reduce waste.

24. D   W2   Supporting Details

According to the passage, Amanda had to look for dripping faucets in her house as part of a school assignment. Answer choice D is correct.

25. C   W4   Paraphrasing/Vocabulary

The word "reduce" means "lower" or "lessen." According to the article, Amanda Carlisle tries to lower the amount of water, food, and other things that she wastes.

26. A   A4   Making Judgments, Drawing Conclusions

Amanda does not seem like the type of person to do something just because everyone else is doing it. The reader knows from the article that Amanda is very serious about wasting as little as she can in her daily life. A lunch box is reusable, so it is a good way to conserve resources. Paper lunch bags are often only used once then thrown in the trash.

27. B   A2   Prediction of Tentative Meaning

The author does not state specifically in the article that what Amanda and her family are doing is hard work, but the reader can infer this from the descriptions of what they are doing.

28. C   A5   Literary Elements and Textual Conventions

Newspaper articles often use direct quotations from people rather than always paraphrasing what people say. This makes the article livelier and more interesting to the reader.

29. **D** W3 Extrapolation of Information

The author is very clear in the article about how Amanda feels about litter and waste. She is also quite outspoken. So, it is likely that she would immediately ask her classmate to pick up the wrapper.

30. Answers will vary.   A1/A4   Questioning, Clarifying, Predicting/ Making Judgments, Drawing Conclusions

Sample answer: When I brush my teeth every night, I keep the water running until I finish brushing. I guess I figure I need to rinse the brush, so I may as well keep the water on. Well, I learned in the article that just one dripping faucet can waste thousands of gallons of water a year. Imagine how much water is wasted when I keep the tap on while I brush my teeth! I am going to make a sign that says "TURN OFF WATER!" and post it on the bathroom mirror. I brush my teeth every night without thinking about the water, so the sign will remind me. Turning off the water is a small thing for me to do, but every little thing counts as far as saving the planet is concerned.

Practice Test 2 Answer Explanations

Writing Task 1

Sample answer:

My favorite time of year is the fall. This is my favorite season for several reasons. First of all, I like the cooler weather because I can wear my favorite sweaters. I also like the way the leaves change color and fall to the ground. I help out at our house raking the leaves. When we are done, we all jump into a big leaf pile!

I like the fall because it is a great time to go to the Terhune Orchards in Princeton. This is a great farm where I go with my family to see the farm animals and to do lots of activities, like walk around the farm trail. On fall weekends, they also have hayrides and a pumpkin patch where we pick our own pumpkins for Halloween.

Halloween is another one of the great things about the fall! We also pick apples and take them home to make applesauce and pies. I love the fall because the weather is so nice and there are so many fun things to do. Don't you think the fall is a great time of year?

"Rosa's New Job"

1. **A** W3 Extrapolation of Information

    After Rosa sighs, she says, "I know, we don't have enough money for this right now." This suggests that Rosa has run into this problem before and knows that her family can't afford it. Answer choice A is correct.

2. **D** A4 Drawing Conclusions

    When Rosa's mother first tells her about the job, Rosa thinks it sounds too easy. However, after chasing Pedro around her grandmother's apartment, she forms the opinion that Pedro is "a monster." Answer choice D is correct.

3. **C** W2 Supporting Details

    Rosa's mother explains that Pedro just has trouble sitting still and suggests that Rosa and Pedro do something that burns off some of his energy. Answer choice C is correct.

4. **B** W1 Theme

    In this story, Rosa gets a job so she can make money to help her family and buy something that she really wants. This shows that she is willing to work hard to reach a goal. Answer choice B is the best answer.

5. **D** W3 Extrapolation of Information

    By the end of the story, you learn that watching Pedro is an exhausting job, even for just a short amount of time. Therefore, you can conclude that Grandma is tired because she chases after Pedro all day. Answer choice D is the best answer.

6. **D** A5 Literary Elements and Textual Conventions

    This phrase compares Pedro to a bolt of lightning. Lightning is fast and often surprising. Given the context of the story, it is clear that Pedro is running around and getting into trouble faster than Rosa can stop him.

7. **B** W4 Paraphrasing, Vocabulary

    Rosa has already tried to do calming, quiet, and imaginative things with Pedro, and nothing has helped. Rosa's mother mentioned that Pedro is a three-year-old who likes to keep moving doing physical things.

8. **C** A2 Prediction of Tentative Meaning

    "You bet" is an expression that means about the same as "of course!" In the context of the story, you can tell that Rosa is starting to have more fun with Pedro because she is doing activities that he likes better. Because Rosa is having more fun and feeling like she is doing a better job, she happily tells Pedro that she'll be back.

9. A W5 Recognition of Text Organization

When Rosa first babysits Pedro, all he wants to do is watch TV or run around the house causing trouble. By the end of the story, Pedro is having so much fun dancing and playing with Rosa that he forgets all about the TV.

10. Answers will vary.   A4   Making Judgments

Sample answer: When Rosa sees the skateboard in the store, she really wants it. However, she knows that her family does not have a lot of money. She decides to get a job so she can make money to buy the things that she wants. This shows that Rosa is both thoughtful and responsible. She is thoughtful because she doesn't beg her mother for the skateboard. She knows that her mother cannot buy it for her. She is responsible because she comes up with a way to make money to buy the skateboard for herself.

Writing Task 2

Sample answer:

My favorite place to be is my tree house. My tree house is in a tree in my backyard. I have to climb a ladder to get into it. I like to go there because it looks out over the whole neighborhood. I can see everyone, but they can't see me!

When I'm in my tree house, I usually read books or just sit and think. Sometimes my friends and I have sleepovers in my tree house. They are a lot fun. My tree house is pretty. The walls are painted blue, and there are curtains on the small window. It smells like pine trees in my tree house.

At night, you can hear all kinds of animals walking around in the woods behind my house. But I feel safe, because my tree house is very high off the ground. My tree house is very peaceful, and that's why I like to go there so much. I think everyone should have a peaceful hideout like my tree house, don't you?

"The Great Car and Dog Wash"

11. A A4   Making Judgments, Drawing Conclusions

At the beginning of the story, Maddie is worried that her brother will see her and tell her to "scram." This implies that her brother does not always want her around.

12. **C**   **W1**   Recognition of a Central Idea or Theme

In the story, Maddie is discouraged because she wants to do something to help the nature preserve. She is not allowed to participate in the car wash because she is "too little." But she and her friend Janine decide to help by washing dogs. The "little" kids in the story make a contribution to the cause.

13. **D**   **A4**   Making Judgments, Drawing Conclusions

Janine first thought of the idea to wash something smaller at the car wash. If Maddie had not called Janine, she probably would not have thought of washing dogs at Ryan's car wash.

14. **C**   **W3**   Extrapolation of Information

You know that Ryan does not always want to play with Maddie, probably because big kids sometimes think that little kids are annoying. But there is also evidence in the story that he likes to play with her sometimes. And at the end of the story, he is obviously proud of his little sister.

15. **A**   **W4**   Paraphrasing, Vocabulary

Maddie has just mentioned something to Ryan that she only could have known if she was eavesdropping on his conversation. People are usually angry when other people eavesdrop on their conversations.

16. **C**   **A2**   Prediction of Tentative Meaning

Janine is so excited about the idea of a dog wash that she shrieks, "you know, I think that might work!"

17. **B**   **A2**   Prediction of Tentative Meaning

Maddie, Ryan, and their friends seem to seriously want to help the Haddonfield Nature Preserve. No one would probably keep the money or claim all the credit. It seems that if one fundraiser was a success, the students will probably raise more money and keep the preserve open.

18. **D**   **A4**   Making Judgments, Drawing Conclusions

Maddie points out in the story that people would be happy to have their dogs washed in the spring because it is so muddy. If the story took place in another season, it is possible that the car and dog wash would not have been such a success.

19. **A**   **A5**   Literary Elements and Textual Conventions

Maddie and Janine probably did have a great time at the car and dog wash, but at the end of the story when they realized that they had done such a great job, they were quite proud of themselves.

20. Answers will vary.   A3/A4   Forming of Opinions/ Making Judgments, Drawing Conclusions

    Sample answer: Ryan's and Janine's ideas for raising money for the nature preserve are both very good ideas. Janine's idea is better because it is more creative. Many students in high school do car washes to make money for something. It is not an unusual idea. Janine is smart because she thinks of something that the younger kids can do at the car wash. Washing dogs while the older kids wash cars is a clever way for the younger kids to pitch in without getting in the way of the older kids or told to "scram."

"A Beginner's Guide to Hamster Care"

21. **A**   W5   Text Organization

    The first paragraph gives an overview of what people need to know before they choose a pet. They need to know how much time they have to care for a pet, as well as what different kinds of pets need.

22. **C**   W2   Supporting Details

    The section titled "What do I need to know?" tells the reader that Syrian hamsters will fight with other hamsters that are in the same cage. The passage does not mention that Syrian hamsters are afraid of other hamsters or that they eat different food from other hamsters. The passage does tell the reader that Syrian hamsters are larger than most other hamsters.

23. **D**   A4   Drawing Conclusions

    The section titled "What does a hamster need?" tells the reader that the spaces between the bars of metal cages might be too large for smaller hamsters. The section tells the reader that plastic and glass cages are sometimes more secure, so smaller hamsters are less likely to escape.

24. **B**   W2   Supporting Details

    The section "Which hamster should I choose?" tells the reader that hamsters sleep during the day and are awake during the afternoon and evening. This means that the hamsters will be livelier during these times and will allow the reader to see what each hamster is like.

25. **C**   W4   Paraphrasing, Vocabulary

    In the same section of the article, the author writes that Syrian hamsters need to be alone in their cages. In contrast, Dwarf hamsters like to be together with other hamsters. People who like the company of other people like to feel close to their friends.

26. **D**   A4   Making Judgments

    The purpose of this passage is to inform the reader of what is required to care for a hamster. The author wants to give the reader the basic information that a beginner would need to care for a hamster.

27. **A**   A4   Making Judgments, Drawing Conclusions

    In the first paragraph of the article, the author states that pets need a lot of time and attention in order to be happy and healthy. You also learn in the article that hamsters need to be played with and fed well in order to be healthy. So, if you don't spend time playing with your hamster and feeding it good food, it will probably get sick.

28. **A**   A5   Literary Elements and Textual Conventions

    Section headings help you find information in a text. In this article, each section provides information that answers the question in the heading. You can find the question that you want answered and read the section to find the answer.

29. **C**   W5   Recognition of Text Organization

    The section "What does my hamster need?" includes all kinds of information about what to buy for your pet hamster, from what kind of cage to choose to what to put in the cage.

30. Answers will vary.   A3   Forming of Opinions

    Sample answer: After reading this article, I think that a hamster would be a great pet for our family. Actually, I think we should get several Dwarf hamsters and keep them together in one glass cage. My family lives in an apartment building, so we don't have a yard. We do have a really good view of the park, though, and our apartment is always filled with light. I think hamsters would be happy in their cage on a table next to the window. They would have a lot to look at when we were not playing with them. Our family does not have enough time to walk a dog several times per day, but my sister and I do have enough time to play with hamsters when we come home from school. We are also vegetarians, which means that we have plenty of leafy greens and other vegetables (and cheese) at home. I think we would enjoy taking care of and playing with Dwarf hamsters very much.

Notes

Notes

Notes

Notes

Notes

Notes